The Shema

Spirituality and Law in Judaism

Books by Norman Lamm

A Hedge of Roses:
Jewish Insights into Marriage and Married Life

The Royal Reach:
Discourses on the Jewish Tradition and the World Today

The Good Society:
Jewish Ethics in Action

Faith and Doubt:
Studies in Traditional Jewish Thought

"Torah Lishmah":
Torah for Torah's Sake, in the Works of Rabbi Hayyim of Volozhin and his Contemporaries

Torah Umadda:
The Encounter of Religious Learning and Worldly Knowledge in the Jewish Tradition

Halakhot ve'Halikhot (Hebrew):
Jewish Law and the Legacy of Judaism: Essays and Inquiries in Jewish Law

The Religious Thought of Hasidism:
Text and Commentary

NORMAN LAMM

The Shema

Spirituality and Law in Judaism

*as exemplified in the Shema,
the most important passage in the Torah*

The Jewish Publication Society
Philadelphia
5761 • 2000

The Jewish Publication Society
2100 Arch Street, 2nd floor
Philadelphia, PA 19103
Composition by VARDA Graphics, Inc.
Design by Serge Lyubomudrov
Manufactured in the United States of America

05 06 07 08 09 10   10 9 8 7 6 5 4 3 2

The Library of Congress has cataloged the hardcover edition of this title as:

Lamm, Norman.
  The Shema: spirituality and law in Judaism as exemplified in
the Shema, the most important passage in the Torah / Norman
Lamm.
      p.   cm.
  Includes index.
  ISBN-10: 0-8276-0655-9 (hc)
  ISBN-13: 978-0-8276-0655-5 (hc)
  ISBN-10: 0-276-0713-X (pb)
  ISBN-13: 978-0-8276-0713-2 (pb)
    1. Shema.   2. Judaism—Liturgy.   I. Title
BB670.S45L36   1998 <Hebr>
296.4´5—dc21   98-40891
                                                     CIP

To the memory of my
beloved mother-in-law
Tillie H. Mehler
(1896–1979),
a person of the highest moral standards,
unusual personal charity,
and genuine "fear of Heaven."
When a stroke robbed her
of the ability to speak,
she still would recite the Hebrew blessings,
and especially the passage of *Shema Yisrael.*

Publication of this book was made possible
by a generous gift from the
Isaac, Doris, and Nina Noinester Foundation

In memory of
Harav Yaakov Leib and Shashka Moinester
Mr. and Mrs. David and Ida Sidewitz
Mrs. Anna Bazer

And in honor of Rabbi Irwin Albert,
Graduate of Yeshiva University, Schoolmate
and Friend of Dr. Norman Lamm

Guardian of Israel,
Guard the remnant of Israel,
And let not Israel perish,
Who proclaim, "Hear O Israel."
                    —*The Daily Prayer Book*

Contents

CONTENTS

Preface

This work began as a series of lectures given at a Senior Honors Seminar at Yeshiva University's affiliated Rabbi Isaac Elchanan Theological Seminary in 1992–1993. My goal was to teach these budding Jewish scholars what they already knew intuitively. I wanted them to be aware of the vaulting role of spirituality in Judaism and of the complex and mutually fructifying relationships between spirituality and Halakha (Jewish law), using the Shema as a detailed illustration of this phenomenon.

A further purpose of that seminar—and this book—was a commentary on the Shema as such. I hoped that some day my students would use this material to convey to many others the ability to recite the Shema in a manner that is spiritually engaging, personally meaningful, and intellectually challenging, and—for those standing outside the Jewish tradition—to acquaint them with some of the scope, profundity, grandeur, and relevance of this simple but eloquent statement of Jewish faith in the oneness of God.

I have added material that has accumulated since then, and as is to be expected, different emphases, foci, and style were inevitable. The spoken word and the written word require different treatment and presentation; furthermore, students are graded by the instructor, whereas the author is graded by his readers. . . .

Most of my students did well in that class. May I fare no worse in the eyes of my readers and, above all, in the eyes of the One whose unity we proclaim thrice daily in the Shema.

Acknowledgments

No book is written and carried through to publication by the author alone; even God availed Himself of the services of Moses and the Elders in getting His book to the world. I therefore take pleasure in acknowledging the following individuals who reviewed the manuscript at different stages of its preparation and graciously offered me their comments and criticisms: my daughters-in-law Rebecca Lamm and Tina Lamm; my nephew Ari Goldman; my friends Dr. David and Phoebe Weisbrot; and my colleagues Dr. Jeffrey Gurock and Dr. Yaakov Elman. I thank them for their kindness and exonerate them from any errors of content or style that may have survived their searching scrutiny.

My greatest debt of gratitude is the one I owe to my editor, Dr. Ellen Frankel of the Jewish Publication Society. I shall not reveal to her my dark thoughts when I saw how extensively and meticulously she marked up my original typescript. But I gladly acknowledge that after the work was done, I began to appreciate her editorial talents, her sensitivity, and her encouragement.

Norman Lamm
New York City
February 11, 1998
15 Shevat 5758

A Note on Translations and Transliterations

I have generally followed the standard Jewish Publication Society translation of the Bible, but I have occasionally permitted myself my own translation; in no case was there a significant difference in meaning.

My use of "He" for God, and occasionally "man" or "mankind" for humanity, are not meant to have any gender significance; I have attempted where possible to be sensitive to such concerns, but I have preferred to avoid stylistic awkwardness even at the expense of offending contemporary codes of "correctness."

My transliterations from the Hebrew generally follow the pattern set by the *Encyclopedia Judaica*.

One last item: I refer to the great R. Moses ben Maimon as "Maimonides," except when the discussion is primarily halakhic, as in the appendix, where I refer to him more appropriately as "Rambam."

The Shema

Hear O Israel: the Lord is our God, the Lord is One
Blessed be His Name whose glorious kingdom
    is forever and ever
And you shall love the Lord your God
with all your heart
and with all your soul
and with all your might.
And these words which I command you this day
shall be upon your heart,
and you shall teach them diligently to your children;
and you shall talk of them
when you sit in your house
and when you walk by the way
and when you lie down and when you rise up.
And you shall bind them for a sign upon your hand,
and they shall be for frontlets between your eyes.
And you shall write them upon the door-posts
    of your house
and upon your gates.

PART I

The First Verse

CHAPTER I

Spirituality, Law, and the Shema

The Shema in Jewish Life

Throughout history, the Shema—the biblical verse, "Hear O Israel, the Lord is our God, the Lord is one" (Deut. 6:4), and the rest of that paragraph (Deut. 6:5–9)—was recited as the dying words of Jewish martyrs, in keeping with the example of R. Akiva who (according to the Talmud, *Berakhot* 61b) uttered the Shema as he was executed by the Romans in the aftermath of the revolt against Rome in the second century C.E. To this day, devout Jews aspire to recite it with their dying breaths. Indeed, it was R. Akiva who interpreted the words of the Shema commanding us to love God "with all thy soul" as "even if He takes thy soul." Later authorities urge that while reciting these words, we should think about our own readiness to submit to martyrdom for the sake of God.[1]

Not only in ancient days but even in our own times Jews, even Jewish children, have appreciated the spiritual significance of the Shema. The following conversation took place in the Warsaw Children's Hospital among Jewish children orphaned from their parents by the Nazis:

> "Well, when my sister died and Mamma carried her out, she didn't have any strength left to go and beg, so she just lay there and cried a bit. But I didn't have any strength to go out either, so Mamma died too, and I wanted to live so terribly much and I prayed like Papa did before, before

they killed him that is. He said: *Shema Yisrael* and I started
to say that too and they came to get the corpses and saw
that I was alive and they brought me here and I'm going to
live."

"Maybe we should say *Shema Yisrael* too?"

The adult who overheard this discussion added, "I didn't
hear any more because I dropped a file and the children fell
silent."[2]

But such dramatic testimony should not be taken as a sign
that the Shema has always been morbidly connected with
death. On the contrary, to profess the unity of God and the love
for God is life affirming; in so doing, we recapitulate the
essence of our spiritual existence under God: to live lives in relative indifference to death.

So central has the Shema been to Jewish identity that it
became the signal for the tragically failed revolt of Jewish
inmates in Auschwitz. In this regrettably little-known incident,
a medallion engraved with the first verse of the Shema was
passed surreptitiously from emaciated hand to hand to trigger
the ill-fated uprising. For the leaders of the rebellion knew that
no Jew would fail to recognize the Shema—the symbol of
Jewish courage, hope, and commitment.[3]

Holocaust historian Yaffa Eliach provides another case in
point:

> After the liberation, an American Jew by the name of
> Lieberman went to Europe, from monastery to monastery,
> from nunnery to nunnery, trying to find Jewish hidden
> children. He would walk into each institution and recite the
> *Shema Yisrael*. Those who responded he would then
> attempt to rescue from the monasteries and nunneries.[4]

Even when all other traces of Jewish identity have been erased, the Shema survives as an after-image on a Jew's memory.

So closely is the Shema tied to Jewish identity that even assimilated Jews, whose relationship to their Jewish heritage is almost completely attenuated, recognize in it their residual link to their people and ancestral faith. When evoked, this vague childhood memory seems to work a special kind of magic on the unconscious.

Many contemporary Jews who do not identify themselves as observant or even as religious nevertheless consider the Shema, when they think about such matters at all, as part of their own heritage. Thus, the Israeli press reported that in the 1996 Israeli elections for Prime Minister, the surprise victory of Benjamin Netanyahu over Shimon Peres was in no small measure the result of the secularist excesses of the liberal Meretz party, junior partners of Prime Minister Peres's Labor party. In particular, one incident offended significant numbers of non-observant and presumably secularist voters: On a flight to Warsaw in 1994, Minister Shulamit Aloni of Meretz objected to then Prime Minister Yitzhak Rabin's intention to include, in a speech he was then crafting, a quotation from the Shema as the affirmation uttered by Jews as they entered the gas chambers. When Aloni's off-the-record comment was reported in the press, it "stuck in the public mind"; many otherwise nonobservant Israelis were outraged.[5] Even for these secular Jews, striking at the Shema was considered viscerally as an attack upon Judaism itself.

The fundamental requirement by the Halakha is for the Shema to be recited twice daily, once in the morning and once after dark. Tradition adds two more times for daily reading of the Shema: once before retiring, at bedside, and once in the preliminary devotions before the morning prayer *(Shaḥarit).*[6]

Spirituality and Law

The Shema has much to tell us about the tension between spirituality and law that lies at the very heart of the Jewish religious enterprise. By "spirituality" I mean the intention we bring to our religious acts, the focusing of our mind and thoughts on the transcendent, the entire range of mindfulness—whether simple awareness of what we are doing, in contrast to rote performance, or elaborate mystical meditations—that spells a groping for the Source of all existence and the Giver of Torah. By "law" I refer to the Halakha, the corpus of Jewish law that has its origin in the Oral Law beginning with Sinai and that was eventually written down in the Mishnah and Gemara—i.e., the Talmud—and codified by later rabbinic authorities.

The contrast between the two—spirituality and law—is almost self-evident. Spirituality is subjective; the very fact of its inwardness implies a certain degree of anarchy; it is unfettered and self-directed, impulsive and spontaneous. In contrast, law is objective; it requires discipline, structure, obedience, order. Yet both are necessary. Spirituality alone begets antinomianism and chaos; law alone is artificial and insensitive. Without the body of the law, spirituality is a ghost. Without the sweep of the soaring soul, the corpus of the law tends to become a corpse. But how can two such opposites coexist within one personality without producing unwelcome schizoid consequences?

Such criticism has a long history. Early Christianity—and later varieties as well, down to our own day—denounced Judaism, as it was being taught and codified and expanded by the great Pharisee teachers, as legalistic and heartless; hence their use of "Pharisee" and "Pharisaic" as terms of opprobrium. In reaction, some defenders of traditional Judaism, exaggerating a valid point to the level of distortion, have focused on Halakha as the totality of Judaism, thus reinforcing the Christian caricature of Judaism.

But such a simplistic dualism misses the point. The life of the spirit need not be chaotic and undisciplined; the life of law, similarly, need not exclude the pulsing heart and soaring soul of the religious individual. In Judaism, spirituality is not antinomian, that is, the opposite of law and a structured approach to our duty under God. Halakha, a "way of life," does not preclude the participation of the heart and a deepening of inwardness. In Judaism, each side—spirit and law—shows understanding for the other; we are not asked to choose one over the other, but to practice a proper balance that respects and reconciles the demands of each.

About a millennium ago, R. Baḥya Ibn Pakuda, *dayyan* (religious judge) and philosopher of Saragossa, Spain, undertook in his *Duties of the Heart* to restore the balance between spirit ("duties of the heart") and law ("duties of the limbs"). At the end of the eighteenth century, a similar but far more controversial effort was undertaken by hasidic masters, such as R. Yaakov Yosef of Polnoye, who were unsparing and acerbic in criticizing their contemporary rabbinic leaders for overemphasizing study and the performance of the commandments, to the exclusion of spiritual participation. And then, as often happens, the pendulum swung to the other extreme; the Hasidim overemphasized spirituality, especially in the sense of ecstasy, at the expense of halakhic correctness. Such excess occasioned reactions from the anti-hasidic rabbinic authorities until a delicate balance was established that did not violate the sensibilities of either group.

To appreciate fully how Judaism has accommodated both spirituality and law within its practice, we can find no better illustration than the teachings pertaining to the proper manner of reading the Shema. Here spirituality defers to law; Halakha dictates such things as the time for the Reading, its language and audibility, and the posture of the reader. In turn, the law not only accommodates but *requires* spiritual intention, i.e., *kavvanah* or meditation, and defines its minimal expression, leaving it up to the spiritual capacity of the reader as to the content and strength of such intention.

Halakha defines at least two levels of *kavvanah*. The most basic is that of the simple awareness that one intends thereby to fulfill a divine commandment. The other is all the rest—the content of the commandment, its religious significance, its spiritual affirmations and commitments, etc. It is this second segment, the meditations recommended, that constitute the element of "spirituality." This is not the spirituality of the "New Age" adherents. The spirituality that emerges from the dialectic between the yearning Jewish soul, questing for holiness, and the discipline and restraint of the Halakha is far different from the amorphous personal enthusiasm and hedonistic religiosity that characterizes so many of the contemporary manifestations of "spirituality." An exposition of the Shema therefore may serve as a paradigm of both the significance of spirituality and the interdependence of spirituality and law in Judaism.

It is in keeping with this goal that this work is written. It is not intended as an historical description of the Reading of the Shema, nor does it in any way presume to be an exhaustive treatment of the subject. In order not to burden the reader with more halakhic material than is necessary for the smooth flow of the text, and yet to accommodate readers more eager for the halakhic dimensions of the Shema, we devote a special appendix to a halakhic analysis of the Shema—its structure and the *kavvanah* that is minimally required. The Book is eclectic in the variety of the sources chosen for presentation and evaluation, drawing on the varied resources of Judaism—Halakha,

Kabbalah, Midrash, Hasidism, the classics of Jewish thought and Jewish philosophy, poetry—as well as modern science and contemporary thought. But despite the variety of references, I hope it will prove coherent in support of its central theses, namely, that the Reading of the Shema exemplifies the daily infusion of spirituality in the life of the observant Jew; that it serves as a paradigm of the creative encounter of spirituality and law in Judaism; and that understanding the Shema in and of itself will make its recitation more meaningful to those who read it as well as to those who stand outside the tradition but wish to understand its central role in Jewish life and thought.

The Shema articulates the first and most fundamental principle, monotheism, that differentiates Judaism from the pagan world—both ancient and modern. Paradoxically, it is regarded as so self-evident that it is only mentioned once in the Torah—in the Shema.[7] So central is this commandment to recite the Shema that R. Judah the Prince, redactor of the Mishnah, chose the Shema as the opening halakha of the entire Talmud. We may therefore conclude that this is the primary halakha and the most fundamental principle of Jewish faith.

The Midrash relates:

> "Hear (*Shema*) O Israel" (Deut. 6:4). Why did [Moses] use the word *Shema*? The Rabbis said: To what may this be compared?—to a king who betrothed a lady with two precious gems. She lost one of them. Said the king to her: You lost one of them, now take good care of the other. So did the Holy One betroth Israel [with two gems]—"We will do (*naaseh*) and we will obey (*nishma;* literally, 'and we will hear')" (Exod. 24:7). They lost one [gem, the *naaseh*, "we will do"] when they made the Golden Calf. Hence, Moses said to them: Now take good care to observe the *nishma* ["we will obey" or "hear"]. Thus: Hear *(Shema)* O Israel. (Deuteronomy Rabbah 3:11)[8]

This midrash is more than a charming homily; it teaches a truly significant idea, namely, that a person's conduct over his lifetime is bound to be defective and wanting. "For there is not a just man on earth that does good and sins not" (Eccles. 7:20). Imperfection is the inescapable lot of humanity; we often do good, but we can never consistently and thoroughly avoid evil. But for two brief periods of the day we do have the opportunity to make up in *nishma* what we so egregiously lack in *naaseh*—that is, in our recitation of the first verse of the Shema and in our *kavvanah,* i.e., the focusing of our attention and intellect on what it is we are saying.

As we shall see, the Halakha never compromised on this principle—as it did, for example, with regard to prayer (by which is meant, technically, the "Eighteen Benedictions," or *Amidah*). There, it first restricted the strict and uncompromising need for *kavvanah* to the first blessing, having despaired of the worshiper's ability to focus his thoughts on what he is reciting during the entire course of the prayer, and eventually abandoned even that minimal requirement because "nowadays" we do not have the capacity for sustained attention for even one short paragraph.[9] This tolerance for the attention deficit of contemporary man was not permitted to affect the law of the Shema; here the Halakha demanded, even after the fact, the need for *kavvanah* in reciting the first verse of the Shema. Indeed, there could not be any compromise in the case of the Shema because of the very nature of the halakhic understanding of the Shema, which insisted upon the integrity of the spiritual dimension of the act.[10] Here is a prime instance where law rises to the defense of spirituality.

We will now turn to our study of the Shema. In the next few chapters, we will discuss in depth the first verse of the Shema, the most significant and triumphant proclamation of Jewish monotheism, focusing especially on the *kavvanah* that ideally ought to inform the meditation of the reader. Afterward, we take up the rest of the first paragraph of the Shema word by word.

It is my hope that these pages will help the reader attain a better appreciation of the elegance of Judaism in achieving a synthesis of law and spirituality, in which neither is compromised and both are enhanced, and in discovering in the six verses of the Shema the secret of its hold over the Jewish religious imagination as well as serving as the source of so much of its creative thinking.

CHAPTER 2

"Hear":
To Listen, To Listen To

The most elementary meaning of the word *shema* is "hear"—the standard translation. It is a summons by Moses to Israel, "Hear O Israel"; so the worshiper summons himself to pay heed to what follows, to "lend an ear" to a significant message that requires his attention.

But the significance of the word *hear* transcends its obvious function as a call to attention or a preface to the rest of the verse. The sense of hearing or listening is in itself of considerable importance. The famous "*Nazir* of Jerusalem," Rabbi David Cohen, colleague and student of Rav Kook, composed a whole volume on this word and its implicit concepts.[1] He contrasts *hearing* with *seeing*, pointing to the Torah's insistence that at Sinai we *heard* God's voice but did not *see* Him (Deut. 4:12–19).[2] Seeing leads to idolatry; the worshiper creates an icon to represent what he saw. Hearing, however, leads to obedience; no physical shape or form beguiles the worshiper. He expresses his devotion in terms of what he has heard, i.e., he obeys the Voice who commands him.

A similar point is made by the former Chief Rabbi of Trier:

> Sound stands nearest to the purely spiritual among the phenomena of the world of the senses. Therefore, God has chosen it to be the medium of sensory revelation. Since what is heard is the least dimensional, it is easier to imag-

ine it as something unlimited, and extendible into infinity, than what is visible or tactile. Sense and spirit mutually interact in hearing.[3]

What was heard at Mount Sinai was not a one-time affair; the voice of God is ubiquitous and continuous. It is up to us to hear it. As R. Joshua b. Levi taught, "Every day a divine voice *(bat kol)* issues from Mount Horeb" *(Avot* 6:2). In the act of hearing we sensitize ourselves to what already exists. It is this hearing, this *shema,* that endows the commandments with "an incomparable vitality and freshness."[4] When we understand the word *shema* in this way, we come up with a novel interpretation of the entire verse: instead of "Hear O Israel, the Lord is our God, the Lord is One," we may now read the verse as, "Hear O Israel the Lord our God: the Lord is One," in the sense of, "Hear the Lord our God, O Israel: the Lord is One."[5]

Similarly, the hasidic master R. Zvi Elimelech Shapira of Dinov, in his classic *Benei Yisasekhar,*[6] distinguishes between faith attained through rational investigation, symbolized by seeing (compare the American colloquial expression, "seeing is believing"), and faith based upon received tradition, represented by hearing; the latter, for the Rabbi of Dinov, is of greater merit and is more enduring.

Not only Jewish scholars but perceptive non-Jews as well have been sensitive to the auditory bias of the Jewish tradition. The Catholic lay theologian Theodore Roszak writes of Jews having acquired "an incomparable ear" in exchange for surrendering their visual and tactile witness:

> [T]hey *heard* . . . they heard as no one else has ever heard. They became history's most alert listeners. Their God was pre-eminently a voice, one who revealed His magisterial presence by speaking into the world from beyond it. . . . Manifested in the image of sound, the divine presence may

span all space, be at once in all places, penetrate all barri-
ers.

Roszak adds: unlike the hypnotic murmur of Hindu and
Buddhist mantra, "the word of the prophetical God instructs;
it is intelligible speech."[7]

The word "hear" implies understanding as well as apperception. In contemporary colloquial English, the expression, "I
hear what you say" acknowledges that the listener has not only
heard the speaker's words but has become aware of the deeper
intention underlying them. Thus, true hearing is cognitive as
well as sensory.[8]

The Talmud accepts both meanings of the word *shema* as the
basis for halakhic rulings on how the Shema is to be recited
(*Berakhot* 13a). Thus, R. Judah the Prince requires that we
must ourselves hear our own enunciation of the first verse of
the Shema. As for understanding what we are saying when we
recite the Shema, the Sages permit the Shema to be read "in any
language that you understand" (*shomei'a,* literally, "hear"),
not only the original Hebrew. The Sages thus agree with
R. Judah but are less strict: if the reciter fails to recite the words
audibly, R. Judah demands repetition of the passage in order to
fulfill the obligation to read the Shema, while the Sages only
advise it strongly but do not disqualify the recitation in the
absence of audibility. The Halakha ultimately decided in favor
of the Sages, and so the preferable translation of *shema* is not
"hear" but "understand." The differing views of R. Judah and
the Sages may also reflect their different judgments as to the
priority of spirituality ("understand," i.e., meditate on the
meaning of what you are articulating) versus law ("hear"—
articulate audibly).

R. Saadia Gaon—who headed the Babylonian academy of
Sura about a millennium ago and whose fame rests upon his

multiple accomplishments as a Talmudist, philosopher, linguist, and translator as well as educator and communal leader—also holds that there are two meanings to the word *shema,* both correct and necessary. The first is familiar to us from the talmudic discussion above: *shema* is synonymous with *da,* "know" or "understand." This meaning is implicit as well in the rabbinic-midrashic interpretation of the biblical expression *naaseh ve'nishma* (Exod. 24:7), "we shall do and we shall understand."[9] The recitation that follows the word *shema* is not a rote recital, a kind of ritualistic incantation, but must be rooted in comprehension.

Saadia's second sense of this word is *kabbel,* "accept," implying faith, commitment, and obedience, as in the talmudic expression for the Shema, *kabbalat 'ol malkhut shamayim,* "the acceptance of the yoke of the Kingdom of Heaven." The recitation is not to be a disembodied intellectual declaration, a mere academic exercise, but must represent a profound spiritual, existential commitment to the content and implications of this first verse of the Shema. That is, we are summoned not only to listen, but to listen *to.*

This element of religious commitment is graphically symbolized in the text of the Torah scroll itself. Scribal tradition prescribes that the last of the three Hebrew letters of the word *shema,* the *'ayin,* be written large. Similarly, the *dalet,* the last letter of the last word, *ehad,* is also enlarged. Two reasons have been offered for these orthographic peculiarities, and both reinforce Saadia's second meaning of *shema,* namely, *kabbel,* "to accept."

The first of these explanations is offered by R. David Abudarham, the fourteenth-century Spanish liturgical commentator: the two letters, *'ayin* and *dalet,* read together, spell *'ed,* the Hebrew word for "witness." To declaim *shema . . . ehad* is to give testimony. Thus, Isaiah proclaims in the name of God, *atem 'edai,* "You are My witnesses" (43:10). It is not enough to know in the sense of understanding with our minds. We must also *make known* by testifying to our faith before God, before our fellow humans, and before ourselves.

The second reason offered for enlarging the *'ayin* and *dalet* is complementary to the first. Not only must we testify to our faith, but we must also guard against betraying it, even inadvertently by hesitation or by hedging our bets. Thus the letter *'ayin* is given prominence in order to distinguish it from an *alef,* which would spell a homonym of *Shema,* sounding similar but meaning something quite different: "maybe" or "perhaps." Similarly, if we were to mistake the *dalet* for its look-alike cousin, *resh,* we might read the final word of the verse as *aher,* meaning "other, another," implying another god, an idol. But when we affirm Judaism's most precious doctrine, the unity of God, we must put aside any theological qualms and accept fully and humbly the sovereignty of the One God. The enlarged *'ayin* and *dalet* caution us to leave our doubts and hesitations for another time and another place.[10]

Our tradition makes room for the honest doubter, for without such doubt questions would never be asked, prejudices never challenged, and science would come to a halt.[11] But when we are seriously engaged in prayer, endeavoring to experience the presence of God, it is not the time to entertain intellectual doubts. In prayer, taught R. Naḥman of Bratzlav, we must cast aside all our "wisdom" and stand before our Maker as children; to be child-like in prayer is as appropriate as to be skeptical in thought. When seeking to wrest transcendent meaning out of existence and to pull ourselves out of the void, we should not cast ourselves into that very void. Rather, at that sacred moment, we can put our doubts aside and, in all integrity, proclaim the unity of God whole-heartedly. (The chronic doubter may achieve the same end—by doubting his doubts.) In an age of skepticism and denial, such unwavering faith is indeed hard to come by even for a short period. But, as a wise hasidic master once said, "even faith requires faith."[12] In the face of all the doubts that plague us, we are invited to believe that we can believe fully and unhesitatingly.

Thus, although the "maybe" and the "perhaps" have their place, the moment of profession of the Shema is not that place. Here, in the inner sanctum of Jewish faith, the 'ayin and dalet are writ large, and the summons is clear: Hear—and commit yourself, O Israel. Da ve'kabbel, as Saadia put it: commit even as you seek to understand.

CHAPTER 3

"Israel":
The People or the Person?

The plain sense of this word in the biblical verse is fairly obvious: "Israel" here refers to the entirety of the people summoned by Moses to hear the proclamation of divine unity. Similarly, when an individual worshiper recites these words, he is making a public proclamation. He thereby testifies to his belief, as it were, before all Israel.

Indeed, the affirmation of divine unity is not a "private" matter between one person and God alone; it is an affirmation by each individual Jew, who in declaring this faith, integrates into *kelal Yisrael*, "the whole community of Israel," as well as into the unbroken continuum of Jewish faith and faithfulness. That is why this verse begins with the word *shema*, "hear," in the singular (rather than *shim'u*, in the plural): the original words were addressed to the entire people of Israel as one, rather than to a mass of individuals.[1]

For another interpretation of "Israel," we turn to a midrash (Deuteronomy Rabbah 2:25) based upon a famous aggada mentioned in the Talmud (*Pesaḥim* 56a), concerning our custom of interjecting, after the first verse of Shema, a line not found in the Bible: *Barukh shem kevod malkhuto le'olam va-ed*, usually translated as "Blessed is the Name of His glorious Kingdom forever and ever." In explaining why this verse has been added to the Shema, the aggada links the Shema to the biblical patriarch Jacob, whose other name was Israel:

"And Jacob called unto his sons and said: gather together that I may tell you what will befall you in the End of Days" (Gen. 49:1). Jacob sought to reveal to his sons the End of Days (i.e., the coming of the Messiah), but the Shekhinah departed from him (and he was unable to prophesy). He said, "Is there perhaps, Heaven forfend, some blemish in my family (that makes me unworthy of receiving the divine message)—such as Abraham, from whom there came forth Ishmael, and my father Isaac, from whom there came forth Esau?" His sons said to him: *Shema Yisrael*, "Hear O Israel (the cognomen of Jacob),[2] the Lord is our God, the Lord is One"; by which they meant to say, "Just as in your heart He is but One, so in our hearts is He but One." Whereupon Jacob declared, "Blessed is the Name of His glorious Kingdom forever and ever."

Said the Rabbis: What practice shall we follow? Shall we recite it? But Moses did not recite it! Shall we not recite it? But Jacob did recite it! Therefore they ordained that it should be recited—but in an undertone. Referring to this aggada, our midrash states:

Wherefrom did the Children of Israel merit [that they should be given the commandment] to read the Shema? When Jacob was about to die, he called his sons together, etc., and they responded, "Hear O Israel, the Lord is our God, the Lord is One." Whereupon he quietly said, "Blessed is the Name of His glorious Kingdom forever and ever."[3]

Alluding to this ancient aggada, an earlier source, the Sifre,[4] notes why Moses summoned the people by the name "Israel," rather than as "children of Abraham, Isaac, and Jacob": Moses specifically invoked Jacob-Israel because of the latter's righteous concern for the spiritual integrity of his family.[5]

Based upon this tradition, another passage in the Midrash (Deuteronomy Rabbah, paragraph 2) draws a parallel between this ancient dialogue between the dying patriarch and his loyal sons and the daily life of the individual Jew. Thus, what applied to the sons of the patriarch applies to us as well:

> R. Levi said:
> And what does Israel (i.e., the Jewish people) say nowadays?—"Hear O Father Israel (i.e., Jacob), we practice that which you commanded us: The Lord is our God, the Lord is one."

According to this midrash, our words, repeated twice daily, are addressed not to the general community, *kelal Yisrael,* but to our very personal, intimate forefather Jacob-Israel. In calling out to him across the chasm of the generations, we assure him and ourselves that the One God he worshiped is ours as well; that we continue his tradition, which he entrusted to his children; that we have not and will not falter as we strive to implement the "Kingdom of Heaven" in our own times and our own places; that three and a half millennia later we still carry aloft our grandfather's torch of *yiḥud Hashem* (the unification of His Name); and that we pledge to continue to do so even in an age of cynicism, confusion, and despair.

CHAPTER 4

"The Lord Is Our God": Names Make a Difference

In the King James Bible, the first verse of the Shema is translated, "Hear O Israel, the Lord our God the Lord is One."

That translation grates on the ear of the contemporary English speaker. Why is the divine Name, conventionally translated in English as "Lord," repeated? The simple answer is that in Hebrew, the copulative verb is understood. Translators must supply it in their own vernaculars. Thus, "*Y-H-V-H Elohenu*" is more accurately rendered, "The Lord *is* our God."

But precisely what does that mean? And what is the difference between these two divine Names?

The Tetragrammaton (the four Hebrew letters *Y-H-V-H*) is ineffable; it is never pronounced as it is written. Indeed, the Talmud held that the proper pronunciation was known only to the priests *(kohanim)* of the Temple in Jerusalem, where the High Priest enunciated it only on one day of the year, Yom Kippur, during the solemn service, as the choir of priests chanted so as to make it impossible for non-priests to hear the Name as it was uttered by the High Priest. The original pronunciation of the Name is lost to us. For liturgical purposes, therefore, the Name is pronounced *as if* it was written *Adonai*, which means, "my Lord." Because of the sanctity of the Tetragrammaton, we do not even pronounce or write *Adonai* except for liturgical or pedagogical purposes; otherwise, we substitute for it yet another euphemism, *Hashem*, which means nothing more than "the Name." It is that term, *Hashem,* that we shall be using in discussing the Shema.

The difference between these two Names—the Tetragrammaton and *Elohim* (translated as "God")—is normally explained in the Jewish tradition as the difference between *middat ha-din* and *middat ha-rahamim,* the attribute of divine judgment (strict justice, wrath, demanding) and that of compassion (love, kindness, forgiving); *Hashem* implies the latter, *Elohim* the former.[1]

For this reason, although we prefer to translate the key verse of the Shema as "Hear O Israel, the Lord *is* our God, the Lord is One," it would be wrong to dismiss the King James translation—". . . the Lord our God the Lord is One"—as simple-minded. That is so because if indeed *Hashem,* "the Lord," represents the personal, relational aspect of Divinity, as opposed to *Elohim,* "God," then the Name designating this divine-human intimacy should be capable of being cast in the possessive case: *my* or *our* Lord, etc. Yet it is only *Elohim* that exists in this form (*Elohenu, Elohekhem,* etc.), not *Hashem,* "the Lord." Therefore, the only way Moses could express the possessive of *Hashem*—the *Jewish* God, as it were, in the sense of personality, intimacy, and involvement in the divine-human dialogue—is by linking it to *Elohim;* hence the compound *Hashem Elohenu,* "the Lord our God." Nevertheless, we prefer—for a variety of reasons—the translation, "the Lord *is* our God."

Of course, these two terms do not represent the measure of God. Other divine attributes coexist with them. Rather, *din* and *rahamim* are emblematic of other pairs of attributes that exist in dialectical relation with each other. Taken together, these pairs of polar opposites give us deeper insight into the comprehensive nature of *yihud Hashem,* the unity of God.

The two Names point to God as seen in Nature versus God as experienced in History. On the one hand, *Elohim* is the Creator, the Master of the cosmos, who both creates and continues to direct the vast symphony of all creation, from the most massive of the galaxies to the tiniest constituent particles of the atom, where matter begins to shade into energy. Thus, the Torah opens: "In the beginning God *(Elohim)* created heaven and earth."

The Name *Hashem,* on the other hand, stands for God as He is revealed in the course of human events. *Hashem* is the Lord of History. As it is written, "And the Lord *(Hashem)* came down upon Mount Sinai" (Exod. 19:20). When *Hashem* "comes down" and involves Himself in human affairs, especially those of Israel, His "peculiar treasure" *(am segula)* chosen for the benefit of all humankind, He does so under the Name *Hashem,* the Lord.[2]

At the most elementary level, *Elohim* is the aspect that God shares with the gods of most of the pagan world as well as with earthly sovereigns, namely, that of (presumed) power or authority. That is why this name as it appears in Scripture is sometimes considered sacred (and hence must not be destroyed or treated with disrespect) and sometimes profane. When it refers to "the Jewish God," it is sacred; when it refers to idols, other deities, or powerful human agencies—that is, to generic aspects of divinity—it is, of course, profane.

Hashem, the Lord, however, is a different matter altogether. This Name belongs to the God known to Jews, who has a special relationship with the Children of Israel. This is the One whom the Jews have chosen to worship as their very own, who has revealed Himself to them and chosen them as His people— the ones who would bear witness to Him and His unity in the world. Thus, the phrase *Hashem Elohenu,* "the Lord is our God," means: just as other peoples have their gods, so do we have ours, personal as well as powerful, intimate as well as sovereign; the One who goes by the Name written as the Tetragrammaton, *Y-H-V-H*, but pronounced only as *Hashem*, "the Lord," literally "the Name," because the correct pronunciation is unknown to us.

At another level, the double name, *Hashem Elohenu*, represents another significant dyad: God's universal as opposed to His national or particularistic aspect. *Elohim* refers to God's universal dimension; *Hashem*, to His very special and particular relation to Israel as the people to whom He has chosen to reveal Himself. Thus, in Scripture, other peoples and their leaders know Israel's God as *Elohim*, whereas Jews (when not estranged from Him, i.e., not under the attribute of *din*, judgment) know God as *Hashem*. Thus, Pharaoh and (more problematically) Balaam, when they refer to Him, or in the rare instances when they encounter Him, speak of *Elohim* (as does the Bible in describing the situation); the only time they use the Name *Hashem* is when they specifically identify "the God of the Jews," without, however, accepting His exclusive authority.

On yet a higher level of abstraction is the distinction between the transcendent and the immanent dimensions of God. *Elohim* refers to the former; *Hashem*, the latter. *Elohim*, the attribute of *din*, God as a generic term, His universal qualities—all this points to a transcendental view of Divinity: God as aloof, beyond, remote. In contrast, *Hashem*—the attribute of *rahamim*, of love and compassion, God's specific relations with Israel, His functioning as the God of a singular nation as well as Sovereign of the cosmos and all humanity—points toward a more immanentist conception: God as available, close to us, involved with us, caught up in a web of relationships with us. Until the advent of human beings in the story of Genesis, the Torah uses no Name other than *Elohim*; only with the appearance of Adam and his developing religious consciousness does the Name *Hashem* emerge—first in conjunction with *Elohim* and then standing by itself.

Of course, all of this can be captured in a more familiar dichotomy: *Hashem* as a personal God, *Elohim* as an impersonal One. By virtue of all we have said about *Elohim*, it is obvious that, in this guise, God is impersonal (or beyond personality) in His role as Creator and in His relation to His non-human creation. At the same time, *Hashem* speaks of personal contact and involvement. God is never to be conceived of as a *person*, yet He does possess *personality;* who can deny Him the very attribute that distinguishes His creatures created in His image?

Various attributes connected to divine acts change in nuance depending on the context of the divine Names. Thus, for instance, the word *tov,* "good," means one thing when used in the context of the natural world created by *Elohim*, another in the context of the historical universe presided over by *Hashem*. The words *ki tov,* "it is good," as they appear in the first chapter of Genesis (e.g., 1:4, "and God saw the light that it was [or is] good") refer to the perfection of the natural order, to God as the One who establishes the organizing principles of the cosmos—the orderly governance of the world, both the power and the limitations of the creation.[3] Contrast this use of *tov* to its connotation in Psalms: "The Lord *(Hashem)* is good to all, and His tender mercies are over all His works" (Ps. 145:9). Here, Scripture alludes to God's goodness in its aspect of *rahamim,* "tender mercies." Unlike its metaphysical connotation in the creation narrative, the word *tov* used in this psalm is much more recognizable to us. We encounter here God's moral goodness; significantly, the name *Hashem* is parallel to God's "tender mercies." This is God who is involved with His creatures, who cares for them, worries over them—in other words, this is the Lord of history whose goodness manifests itself in the affairs of humankind.[4]

The two divine Names draw to themselves separate clusters of ideas and nuances, like a magnet attracting iron filings around its opposite poles. On the one hand, *Elohim* is God's generic name. It represents *din,* judgment; His universal aspects; His transcendence; His impersonal attributes; His role as Creator; and His metaphysical goodness. *Hashem,* on the other hand, is God's "Jewish name," associated with mercy and love; His specific adoption by the Children of Israel as their own God; the particularistic dimensions of that relationship; His immanence; His personal and relational qualities; His role as the Lord of History; and the Source of moral goodness, the Revealer of Torah.

These distinctions were never meant to imply different *essences,* that is, beings ontologically independent of each other, for that would border on idolatry. No, in the end "the Lord is One"; the distinctions are solely in the eyes of the human beholder and must never be ascribed to God. The two poles, however we define them, are complementary, never contradictory. The ancient world, however, often regarded these two poles as conflicting with each other rather than representing different aspects of one reality. In the cultures surrounding Israel, polytheistic and dualistic religions abounded. The Zoroastrians of Persia posited a god of light and goodness, and another of evil and darkness. It was in order to counter this form of paganism that the prophet Isaiah characterized Israel's God as the One who proclaims "I form the light and create darkness; I make peace and create evil" (Isa. 45:7). Early Christianity, too, had to contend with heretical sects such as the Manicheans, who saw life in starkly dualistic terms. In such heresies, "Satan" was regarded as a real and independent power over and against God, rather than as a symbol or metaphor of evil.

This virus of dualism still infects humankind even today. Our metaphysical and psychological limitations incline us toward a fragmented philosophy in which the world is conceived of in over-against terms. This is, of course, not an altogether bad thing. It is the very stuff of analysis, without which neither philosophy nor science can make much headway. As the Sages put it, *im ein da'at havdalah minayin;* without understanding no distinctions can be made. And the converse is true as well: in the absence of distinctions there is a dearth of understanding. But when we impose this fractionated vision onto our religious quest and conceive of the duality as ontological, that is, as possessing ultimate reality, we flirt with paganism.[5]

The Torah—recognizing that our reason inclines toward dualism even when contemplating our own Creator—affirms in the Shema that all such dichotomies and distinctions are purely subjective, expressive of our human limitations. Beyond all such divisions there is but one objective Reality: God is One.

Finally, we come to still another shade of meaning pertaining to the Tetragrammaton in the first verse of the Shema: the element of divine lordship, God's mastery and sovereignty in the world. The English translation of the Tetragrammaton as "Lord" is only approximate, representing a direct translation of the Hebrew euphemism *Adonai,* literally, "my Lord." However, this substitute term has no necessary connection to the ineffable Tetragrammaton.

But is it really so arbitrary a substitution? The Halakha offers us an interesting commentary on the matter: The Babylonian Talmud (*Ḥagigah* 4a) teaches that a slave is exempt from the law of *re'iyah,* that is, the requirement to make the pilgrimage to Jerusalem and attend the Holy Temple during the three major festivals. Why this exemption? Because the relevant verse in Scripture reads, "Three times in the year all your males shall appear before the *Lord* God" (Exod. 23:17). The word for "Lord" here is *adon,* which is quite literally "master" or "lord." The Talmud adds, "This refers to one who has only one *adon;* but this one (i.e., the slave) has another *adon.*" Thus, only a free man—one who has but one Master, the Creator— is obligated to make the pilgrimage to the Temple. This sacred duty is reserved for those who acknowledge but one Master.

The Jerusalem Talmud similarly interprets the first verse of the Shema:

> How do we know that a slave is exempt from the obliga- tion to recite the Shema? For it is written, "Hear O Israel, the Lord is our God, the Lord is one"—this refers to one who has no other *adon* other than the Holy One. This therefore excludes the slave who has more than one *adon.* (J. *Berakhot* 25a)[6]

Therefore, the standard English translation of the Tetragram- maton as "Lord" is indeed quite apt. And so, the Shema can be seen as a clarion call for human freedom under God's sover- eignty. It is to be recited only by one "who has no master other than God." And in reciting the first verse of the Shema, we thereby proclaim our spiritual dignity: we affirm the oneness of God as free men and free women, for God is our one and only *adon.*

CHAPTER 5

"The Lord Is One":
The Eschatological Interpretation

[handwritten: Reading w/ end of time messianic age / death]

These two words—*Hashem eḥad,* "the Lord is One"—constitute probably the most significant and revolutionary phrase in the entire lexicon of Jewish thought. Simple yet enormously complex, they have challenged and stimulated generations of scholars and ordinary folk since they were first uttered by Moses toward the end of his days. In exploring the various interpretations of these two critical words, we gain valuable insights into the content of Judaism's major proclamation of faith.

Rashi (to Deut. 6:4), apparently troubled by the repetition of the Name *Hashem,* "the Lord," in the Shema, comments:

> The Lord who is our God now, but not (yet) the God of the (other) nations, is destined to be the One Lord, as it is said, "For then will I give to the peoples a pure language, that they may all call upon the name of the Lord, to serve Him with one consent" (Zeph. 3:9). And (likewise) it is said, "And the Lord shall be king over all the earth; on that day shall the Lord be One and His name One" (Zech. 14:9).

Thus, the mention of the first two divine Names—*Hashem* and *Elohim/Elohenu*—evokes the current condition of monotheism, when only Israel fully accepts the utter unity of God; the repetition of *Hashem* in the final phrase, "the Lord is One," refers to the End of Days, the very distant future, the time of the coming of the Messiah and the resurrection of the dead, when this great faith will be accepted by *all* humanity.

Rashi's source for his comment is found in the Sifre (to *Va-et'ḥanan*, 31):

> Why does the verse say, "the Lord is our God"? Does it not state (later in the same verse) "the Lord is One"? . . . Another interpretation: (it is intended) for all human beings. (Thus:) "the Lord is our God"—in this world; "the Lord is One"—in the world-to-come (i.e., the Messianic era, when His unity will be universally acknowledged). Therefore is it said, "And the Lord shall be king over all the earth; on that day shall the Lord be One and His name one" (Zech. 14:9).

The Sifre ponders two reasons for the second mention of *Hashem:* one universal, the other eschatological. But exactly what is meant by affirming the *future triumph* of Judaism's *present faith?*

Because of America's climate of cultural and religious pluralism, we commonly take this declaration to mean that Jews will someday be free to observe their faith in its fullest sense and that all other peoples will acknowledge the rightness of Judaism's fundamental principles and purify their own religions to believe in the oneness of God without compromise, even while they express this purified faith in their own idiom and form of worship. The source for this interpretation is generally given as Micah (4:5): "For let all the peoples walk each one in the name of its god, but we will walk in the name of the Lord our God for ever and ever."[1] In halakhic terms, this means that all non-Jews will accept the Noahide Laws (the "Seven Laws of the Children of Noah," the Torah's legislation of the basic moral and religious code for all humankind) and

settled nations

formally become *gerei toshav,* halakhically recognized "resident aliens."

At the end of his *Mishneh Torah,* Maimonides takes this eschatological vision one step further:

> That which Isaiah said, "And the wolf shall dwell with the lamb, and the leopard shall lie down with the kid" (Isa. 11:6), is a parable and a puzzle. Its meaning is this: that Israel will dwell securely with the wicked of the pagan nations who are compared to wolves and leopards . . . and they will all return to the true faith and will no longer rob and destroy; rather, they will peacefully eat permissible foods as do Israelites. (*Hilkhot Melakhim,* 12:1)

One contemporary scholar[2] maintains that the words, "and they will return to the true faith," clearly imply the conversion of the entire world to Judaism.[3] Indeed, that seems clearly to be Maimonides' intent when he states that the entire world will adopt a kosher food diet!

But whatever the ultimate goal for humanity—whether pure monotheism, even if associated with a non-Jewish cult (possibly Micah's theme); or the status of resident aliens *(gerei toshav);* or the conversion of all humankind to Judaism (Zephaniah and Maimonides)—the interpretation suggested by the Sifre adds two significant elements to our understanding of the Shema.

The first, to which we shall return later, is that the oneness of God is, as it were, still fractured or incomplete. The divine *Name* is not yet one (names, especially divine Names, are charged with enormous metaphysical significance in the Torah); only in the distant future will God's unity be acknowledged. Indeed, the Kabbalah teaches that God is dependent, as it were, upon human beings to establish His Kingdom. (This is reminiscent, of course, of the doctrine of "the breaking of the vessels," the primal cosmic cataclysm at the heart of the Lurianic creation drama, which must be "repaired" by means of the "elevation" or "redemption" of the divine sparks that inhere in matter.[4] Similarly, it is up to us to "elevate" or "redeem" the holy sparks that inhere in the coarse "shells," trapped there after "the breaking of the vessels." The divine unity is imperfect until that happens; the "reputation" of the Creator is sullied and His Name is not One unless and until mankind as a whole acknowledges the divine unity.)

The Maharal teaches that "there is no king without a people."[5] It is *we*, mere mortals though we be, who manifest God's sovereignty. It is *we* who bring about His "Kingdom of Heaven." Therefore it is we who restore and complete His unity. That unity is flawed or incomplete because it is not yet universally acknowledged. In proclaiming our confidence that the wholeness of that divine oneness will yet be restored, we commit ourselves to *bring about* that situation of redemption. As Saadia maintained about the double meaning of the word *shema*: we not only acknowledge but commit ourselves (*da*, "know, understand"); and, in taking upon ourselves the *kabbalat 'ol malkhut shamayim* (the "acceptance of the yoke of the Kingdom of Heaven"— *kabbel*, "accept, commit yourself"), we not only submit to the divine Lordship over us, which is expressed in a life of Torah and mitzvot, but we also resolve to widen the circle of those who accept Him so that, ultimately, all humankind will declare that God is One.

Here lies an answer to those Jews, deeply committed to their Judaism, who often pose the challenge, usually with a degree of petulance: Does it really matter what the Gentiles believe? Do we—and should we—have any interest in their religion, their theology? The answer is, obviously, that we should and we must. Nothing short of God's ultimate unity depends on how and to what extent we encourage all of humankind to acknowledge that unity and the consequences, especially moral, of that belief. We are, in this sense, responsible for them.[6] A truly religious Jew, devoted to his own people in keen attachment to both their physical and spiritual welfare, must at the same time be deeply concerned with all human beings. Paradoxically, the more particularistic a Jew is, the more universal must be his concerns.

Surprisingly, this universalist element often emerges where we least expect it—such as in the writings of one of the most radical hasidic masters, R. Naḥman of Bratzlav.[7] The Bratzlaver interprets two of the talmudic laws relating to the Shema as prescriptions to implementing this universalism. About the halakha, "'Hear'—any language that you can hear (i.e., understand)" (the Talmud's warrant for permission to recite the Shema in any language),[8] he teaches that this law implies the proclamation of divine unity to *all* humanity; and the halakha "let your ear hear what your mouth says" (normally understood as requiring that the reading of the Shema be audible to one's own ears), implies that such relatedness to the Creator already exists in the world and needs only to be revealed: "That is, one can reveal His blessed divinity even in the languages of the pagan nations."

The theme of divine unity now leads us to another, related theme of both religious and historical significance. Our success or failure in discharging our responsibility to establish *yiḥud Hashem,* the unity of God, is a matter of the "sanctification of the Name" *(kiddush Hashem)* or its "desecration" *(ḥillul Hashem)*—an exceedingly important pair of concepts in Jewish law, lore, and history. If, through our persuasiveness—or, more importantly, our example as believers in and practitioners of Judaism, as the people of Torah—we incline the non-Jewish world to a greater respect for Torah and Judaism, and hence to a more refined notion of *yiḥud Hashem,* then we have "sanctified" the Name, the very Name that is now fragmented and fractured but that will, through such sanctification, become whole again: "And the Lord shall be king over all the earth; in that day shall the Lord be One *and His Name One.*" If we fail, we desecrate the Name, condemning it to continue in its present state of impairment and imperfection.

In another biblical verse beginning with the words *Shema Yisrael* (there are only four such verses in all), we find an interesting connection drawn between "sanctification of the Name" and *yiḥud Hashem.* Maimonides makes the following comment on the verse commanding the *kohen mashuaḥ milḥama* (the priest-chaplain), on the eve of battle, to address the army of Israel, saying, "Hear O Israel, you are drawing near to battle against your enemies" (Deut. 20:3): "He must know that he does battle for the sake of the unity of God *(yiḥud Hashem)* . . . and his intention must be only to sanctify the Name of the Lord" (*Hilkhot Melakhim,* 7:15).[9] Thus, the notion of unifying God's Name through our own actions predates and extends beyond the Kabbalah. It is part of the mainstream rabbinic tradition as well: an unredeemed world both reflects and causes the unredeemed state of divinity. This idea is at the heart of the Kaddish prayer, "May the great Name be magnified and sanctified": we here acknowledge that the divine Name itself is in need of fulfillment and sanctification.[10] The Jewish people can help achieve this cosmic sanctification by fulfilling our duties of obedience by means of performing the mitzvot and studying the Torah. And the Creator can do His part by redeeming Israel and thus vindicating His promise.

The second element that the Sifre's view contributes to our understanding of the Shema is that of the coming of the Messiah—which follows logically from the premise of the broken nature of divine unity in our present predicament. It adds the dimension of hope to that of faith, of aspiration to that of affirmation. By introducing this eschatological note into the very heart of the Shema, the Sifre places the Messianic belief front and center in Jewish doctrine.[11]

CHAPTER 6

"The Lord Is One": All and Only

All: The Comprehensiveness View

The Sifre, as we have seen, reserves for Israel alone the full commitment to *yiḥud Hashem* and considers the universal acceptance of divine unity a matter of eschatological realization: only in the Messianic era will all humankind acknowledge the oneness of God. The Talmud, however, takes our central verse, "Hear O Israel," more literally, interpreting it as affirming the comprehensive divine unity without making a distinction between the days of the Messiah and our own time:

> R. Jeremiah was once sitting before R. Ḥiyya b. Abba, and the latter saw that [R. Jeremiah, who was reading the Shema,] was prolonging (the word *eḥad,* "one") very much. He said to him: Once you have declared Him king over [all that is] above and below and over the four corners of the heaven, no more is required (*Berakhot* 13b).[1]

The content of R. Ḥiyya's recommended *kavvanah* is clear: the sovereignty of God at all times, present as well as future.

Thus, whereas the Sifre sees a fragmented unity now and holds out hope for full unity only at the End of Days, the Talmud makes no mention of the distant future but maintains that divine unity is complete even in the present.

Which view is "correct"? Which *kavvanah* is to be preferred in practice? Further, why did R. Ḥiyya b. Abba object to more than the minimum meditation?

Immediately before the above passage about R. Jeremiah and R. Ḥiyya, the Talmud records:

> Symmakhus says: Whoever prolongs the word *eḥad* has his days and years prolonged. R. Aḥa b. Jacob said: [He must dwell] on the *dalet*. R. Ashi said: Provided he does not slur over the *ḥet*.

(The two letters mentioned, *dalet* and *ḥet,* refer to their preceding vowels in the word *eḥad,* not to the consonants themselves. Thus, R. Aḥa b. Jacob recommends lengthening the second syllable of *eḥad,* and R. Ashi cautions against a resultant tendency to shorten or slur over the first syllable.)[2]

Rabbenu Yonah[3] elaborates:

> He should prolong the *dalet* until he meditates that the Creator of the world is king above and below, in heaven and on earth and its four corners, east and west and north and south, in the great abyss, and in his own 248 organs. But if he cannot keep so much in mind, he should think: the Lord who is now our God will one day be One (for all the world).[4]

Thus, R. Yonah prefers the Talmud's recommendation over that of the Sifre, but the latter is permissible in the event of need or exigency.

But we are still left with an apparent disagreement between our two major sources. R. Ḥiyya b. Abba's decision in the Talmud that "no more is required" indicates that he considers his recommended meditation as the maximum. To add to it an eschatological meditation, even in case of need, i.e., lack of time or learning, is not allowed.

However, this apparent contradiction between the Talmud and the Sifre disappears if we consider a slight variant to our printed talmudic text. The version recorded by R. Isaac Alfasi gives us new insight into which *kavvanah* is appropriate for the first verse of the Shema. The text according to Alfasi reads:

> R. Jeremiah was once sitting, etc. [R. Ḥiyya b. Abba] said to [R. Jeremiah]: Why so long? Said [R. Jeremiah]: what then [is the proper length of meditation]? Said [R. Ḥiyya b. Abba]: So that you declare Him king over heaven and earth and over the four corners of the world.

What is significant here is the added bit of dialogue missing in the standard text: R. Ḥiyya b. Abba asks R. Jeremiah why he is taking so much time reading the Shema, and he replies: what then? To which R. Ḥiyya b. Abba responds, "So that" (rather than "Once you have"), etc., as if to say: whatever thoughts are running through your mind at this time, they should not exceed the time it takes to meditate on the divine sovereignty over heaven and earth in all directions. Hence, in this variant of our text, the question is not *what* to meditate on, but for *how long;* for by spending too much time on the first verse of the Shema, one thereby imposes upon others in the congregation *(tirḥa de'tzibbura),* distracting those who may not have the capacity for or interest in more extended meditation.[5] Alternatively, R. Ḥiyya may be cautioning against *yuhara,* excessive pride in performing religious obligations.[6]

Interpreted this way, the two texts do not conflict with each other and thus require no resolution. The Talmud text simply recommends that *a* meditation—not one specific meditation— be considered the time limit to finish reciting the word *eḥad.* We are free to choose, for that meditation, from among a number of interpretations of our critical verse; those mentioned in the Sifre and Talmud are but two of many. A number have been proposed by more recent authorities.[7]

Some of these interpretations follow the Talmud's lead in focusing on divine omnipresence: God's unity suffuses all of space so that, in the words of the Zohar, *let atar panui mineih,* "there is no place that is without Him"—above, below, indeed everywhere. No place is without God—but what of time? Does God fill all eternity as well?

Rav Kook[8] infers this aspect from our talmudic passage. Apparently following Rashi rather than *Talmidei R. Yonah* in limiting the entire talmudic meditation to the *dalet,* the last syllable of *ehad,* he locates an interpretive vacuum in the Talmud's exhortation, "as long as he does not slur over the *het.*" What, if anything, must we bear in mind while reciting that first syllable? Rav Kook's answer is that *het,* the eighth letter of the Hebrew alphabet (with the numerical value of eight), represents the seven days of the week—a human cycle of time—and "what is above it," i.e., seven plus one. Thus, eight is a symbol of eternity. Therefore, for Rav Kook, the *het* represents God's unity throughout all time: both mundane time and eternity. The unity of God, then, not only encompasses all space, but all time as well: God is One both in our time and beyond all time.[9]

We now turn to three cases, all found in the prayer book, where the Shema is placed in eschatological contexts. In the daily morning service, after the recitation of the Song at the Red Sea (Exod. 15:1–20), the section concludes with our verse from Zechariah, "And the Lord will be king over all the earth," etc. In some versions, this is followed by: "And in Your Torah it is written, Hear O Israel, the Lord is your God, the Lord is one." This same passage is often appended as well to the *Alenu* prayer that marks the formal end of every service. So, too, at the end of *Malkhuyot* (Kings), the first of the three major sections of the

Rosh Hashanah *Musaf* service, this same passage concludes a sequence of verses on the theme of divine sovereignty[10]—again, suggesting an intimate bond between the Shema's proclamation of divine unity and Judaism's eschatological vision.

In particular, the two paragraphs of the *Alenu* prayer encapsulate the two interpretations of divine unity in the Shema: the comprehensive and the eschatological.

The first paragraph, *Alenu le'shabe'ah,* expresses in spirit the talmudic view: God is the exclusive One to whom all praise is due and who "abides" everywhere: "in heaven above and earth below." Although it does not explicitly deny an eschatological vision, it makes almost no mention of the other (pagan) nations of the world or their ultimate fate except in a negative sense: "for He has not made us like unto them," etc. Rather than project its vision into the future, it focuses on God's comprehensive unity here and now.

In contrast, the second part of the prayer, *Al ken nekaveh,* emphasizes the themes we have associated with the Sifre: an eschatological, universalist vision of the End of Days when idolatry and paganism will be banished and all humans will turn to God, and the divine kingdom will exercise exclusive control over all the universe. Furthermore, we find an explicit link to the very heart of the Shema through the notion of *kabbalat 'ol malkhut shamayim,* "the acceptance of the yoke of the Kingdom of Heaven," for the paragraph with the key verse of Zechariah, "And the Lord will be king over all the earth," etc.

Thus, just as the universalist and particularist emphases, reflected both in the two divine Names in the Shema as well as in the two blessings preceding it, are complementary to each other rather than in conflict, so too with the two rabbinic meditations suggested as appropriate when reciting the first verse of the Shema as well as the two paragraphs of *Alenu* and *Al ken nekaveh:* whether we contemplate God's sovereignty in the

43

context of infinite space and time or in the context of the End of Days, we are still rendering homage to the One.

Only: The Exclusivist Interpretation

A number of Rishonim—Rashbam, Ibn Ezra, and Albo among others—offer yet a third and the most concise definition of *ehad*. God is one in the sense of *levado*: He *alone* is God. A later authority, Shadal (R. Samuel David Luzzatto, nineteenth-century Italy), connects this particular interpretation to the following verse: "You shall love the Lord your God with all your heart and all your soul and all your might." That is, because Y-H-V-H is the only God, therefore you shall love Him with *all* your heart and soul and might. You do not have to share that love for Him with other gods. The well-known neo-Kantian philosopher, Hermann Cohen, presents an even more intense form of this same concept of *ehad* as "the one and only" Deity. Cohen translates God's oneness as *Einzigkeit* (uniqueness) rather than as *Einheit* (oneness).[11]

One of the earliest sources to suggest this exclusivist definition of *ehad* is the Mekhilta, an ancient midrash on the Book of Exodus (*Ba-hodesh, 5*). On the opening words of the Ten Commandments, "I am the Lord your God," the Mekhilta comments that these words were proclaimed in order to discredit polytheism. For though God appears in different guises, He remains the One and Only God. Thus, "'I am the Lord your God'—the same One who was in Egypt, at the Red Sea, at Sinai, in the past and in the future, in this world and in the world-to-come." The Mekhilta concludes by invoking a verse from Isaiah (44:6), "Thus says the Lord king of Israel and its Redeemer, the Lord of hosts, 'I am first and I am last and besides Me there is no god.'"

We also find support for this exclusivist interpretation of divine unity in the term *yiḥud Hashem,* commonly translated as God's unification. Why *yiḥud* and not *aḥdut,* "unity," from the word *eḥad?* Setting aside the more mystical teachings of the Kabbalists regarding *yiḥud Hashem,* we can draw a convincing parallel from the paradigm of human marriage. The Talmud (*Kiddushin* 6a), discussing the laws concerning the key word *mekudeshet* in the conventional marriage formula, *harei at mekudeshet li,* "you are hereby betrothed *(mekudeshet)* to me," asks: which synonyms of this word are valid and which are invalid for use in betrothal? One of the terms considered is *meyuḥedet,* a transitive verbal form of *yiḥud.* Since *meyuḥedet,* like *mekudeshet,* denotes setting aside or designating for a special purpose, is it a legally proper term for effecting marriage?[12]

Although the Talmud fails to resolve this question conclusively, it is significant that the term *meyuḥedet* is proposed as the equivalent of *mekudeshet.* Now, since the husband designates his wife as *meyuchedet* (set aside for him), he thereby becomes her *yaḥid,* her only beloved. In the essential structure of the Halakha, polygamy is not considered adultery and was banned by special edict for Ashkenazi communities only about a thousand years ago; polyandry has never been permitted. So too, *yiḥud Hashem* means not only that we set God for us, but that *we submit to being set aside by Him,* that we participate existentially in the acknowledgment of his *aḥdut,* His exclusive claim on us.

Thus, *yiḥud Hashem* is the human component of *aḥdut Hashem.*

CHAPTER 7

"The Lord is One": Kabbalistic Interpretations

Before moving on to kabbalistic views of divine unity, let us first summarize the three main lines of interpretation of our key word, *eḥad*. The third leader of the Ḥabad movement in Hasidism, R. Menaḥem Mendel of *Lubavitch,* provides us with a concise formulation. He points to three successive interpretations of the oneness of God. First and most obvious is that there exist no other gods—the simplest and most direct expression of monotheism. Taking this basic proposition one step further, the medieval Jewish philosophers understood God's unity as *uniqueness,* a difference in quality as well as in number: God is utterly incomparable and hence ultimately unknowable. The last stage of interpretation was articulated by the Besht and his disciples, especially the "Great Maggid," R. Dov Ber of Mezerich, and most elaborately developed by R. Shneur Zalman of Liady, the founder and first leader of Ḥabad. We now turn to this mystical approach, beginning with the comments of the Zohar, the foundational document of Kabbalah.

Immediately after the first verse of the Shema, tradition interjects a sentence that, as mentioned earlier, is not found in the Bible at all. The phrase *Barukh shem kevod . . .* ("Blessed is the Name of His glorious Kingdom forever and ever") was introduced here because of the tradition concerning Jacob and his sons.[1] The verse has much to teach us about the meaning of *eḥad* in the opening verse of the Shema.

What, other than this ancient aggada, connects the first verse of the Shema to the non-biblical addition, *barukh shem kevod?*

The Zohar (I, 18b) characterizes the first verse of the Shema as *yiḥuda ila'ah* (the "Higher Unification") and *barukh shem kevod malkhuto le'olam va-ed* as *yiḥuda tata'ah* (the "Lower Unification"). In hasidic literature, we find two widely divergent interpretations of these Zoharian terms as applied to the two opening verses of the Shema, each of which derives from two fundamentally different conceptions of divine unity.

On one side, we find an unexpected alliance between two ideological antagonists, R. Shneur Zalman, founder of the Ḥabad movement in Hasidism and author of the *Tanya,* and R. Ḥayyim Volozhiner, founder of the famed Yeshiva of Volozhin and leading spokesman of the Mitnagdim (opponents of Hasidism), whose ideas are spelled out in his *Nefesh ha-Ḥayyim.* Their interpretation of the Shema might be labeled the *radical* or *acosmic* view. Opposing them is the hasidic zaddik, R. Zvi Hirsch of Ziditchov, author of *Sur me-Ra va-Aseh Tov,* whose view could be called the *moderate* or *cosmic-affirming* view.

R. Shneur Zalman and R. Ḥayyim hold that *yiḥud Hashem* implies not only that no other gods exist, i.e., the absence of multiplicity, but also that *nothing else can be said truly to exist.* They interpret quite literally the verse, "Know therefore this day and consider it in your heart that the Lord is God in heaven above and upon the earth beneath; *ein 'od,* there is no other" (Deut. 4:39); to these last two words they append *mammash,* "literally." In other words, the world, in the face of God, is reduced to nothingness; it is unreal and vanishes into nonexistence. This radical denial that the cosmos really exists is known as *acosmism* or as *illusionism* because its proponents aver that the world is only an illusion. It pushes the word *eḥad,* "one," to its ultimate limits—and perhaps beyond them . . .

Thus, R. Shneur Zalman writes in *Tanya* (2:6): "For the physical world too, which appears to the eye as utterly substantial, is literally nothing and naught compared to the Holy One." And R. Ḥayyim writes similarly in *Nefesh ha-Ḥayyim* (3:2): "'There is no other' other than Him [must be taken] literally: there is nothing at all in all the worlds . . . such that you may say that no created object and no world exist; rather, all is filled with the simple essence of His oneness." In other words, the mundane realm is an illusion. Only God truly exists; all else is His dream, as it were. *Therefore* is He called *eḥad*, One. This notion, they maintain, is the true meaning of the first verse of the Shema, what the Zohar calls the "Higher Unification."

What we have here is a highly abstract, esthetically beautiful, and conceptually compelling understanding of God's unity, one that goes far beyond the categories of "one" proposed by Aristotle and later developed and transmuted by medieval Jewish as well as non-Jewish theologians.[2] For what can be more truly and thoroughly "one" than that unity outside of which nothing at all exists? This philosophical idea, based upon a mystical intuition, elevates the unity of God beyond all normal conceptions of oneness to its most absolute form. In this purest notion of unity, transcendence itself is transcended, and the One and the All and the Nothing meet in what is truly the "Higher Unification."[3]

But this idea, abstract and sophisticated as it is, poses an enormous challenge to the very foundations of halakhic life. For Torah and Halakha are based upon an assumption that lies at the very heart of the Jewish religious enterprise: that there is a "real" world, a vast whirling conglomeration of actual substances, a universe of discrete weights and measures, a realm that is as real as the nail in one's shoe. How shall we distinguish between right and wrong, innocent and guilty, kosher and non-kosher, pure and impure, holy and profane, and all other such clear and measured halakhic categories if what we are dealing with is unreal, a mere illusion, a dream of God? If nothing truly exists, what is Torah all about? Is not this mystical intuition in total conflict with fundamental halakhic assumptions?

The problem goes even deeper than Halakha. For if all the world is an illusion, of what value are life and love and hope? Why should we strive for success and aspire to transcend the bounds of self? Why even yearn for religious experience itself? If we are but actors in Someone Else's dream, how can we make sense of sacrifice and suffering, of pleasure and happiness, of the myriad emotions and sentiments that both inspire and agitate us? Why exercise moral restraint and try to achieve a minimum of human dignity? If I am unreal, aren't my most vital concerns and most sacred values, my most precious loves and relationships equally unreal? How then do I make sense of a life that hangs on the gossamer threads of illusion?

The answer that R. Shneur Zalman and R. Ḥayyim propose is that it is *God's will* that we act *as if* the world were real, that we take God's dream as our reality. Indeed, they argue that this very idea is the message of *Barukh shem kevod*. For complementing the "Higher Unification" expressed in the first verse of the Shema is the "Lower Unification" expressed by *Barukh shem kevod*. This verse confirms the cosmos not as ultimate reality but as the divinely willed reality. And this pseudo-real world that we accept as real because we are so commanded is the *malkhut*, "kingdom," of the Creator. In it, faced with a stunning plethora of phenomena of the most varied sorts, a world in dialogue with its Creator, we proclaim that God is One, and we bless His glorious kingdom forever and ever.

In other words, the first verse of the Shema articulates the "Higher Unification," the radical notion that God is One because nothing else exists; the *Barukh shem kevod* expresses the more conventional interpretation of divine unity as giving rise to a divinely approved and willed sacred fiction, namely, what we experience as our real existence.

How can two such widely divergent and apparently contradictory ideas be reconciled? To resolve this paradox, both R. Shneur Zalman and R. Ḥayyim point to a significant dichotomy proposed by the great sixteenth-century Safed Kabbalist, R. Moshe Cordovero, who described two radically different ways of perceiving the world: "from His side" and "from our side." Extrapolating from Cordovero's teaching, they explain that the "Higher Unification" can only be perceived from the divine perspective; the "Lower Unification," from our human perspective. From the point of view of the *Ein Sof*, God in His aspect of utter transcendence, nothing exists but divinity; all else is fantasy, chimerical, illusory. "'There is no other'—literally." But from our limited human point of view, the world is not a dream, not even a divine dream; it possesses ontological validity. We treat it as real and autonomous. It is within this context that we conduct our dialogue with the Creator.[4]

Hence, when we recite the Shema, what we must meditate on is this two-part notion that the "Higher Unification," is "from His side," while the "Lower Unification" is "from our side." *This must be our* kavvanah, *what we must bear in mind with all the powers of concentration at our command, when we recite the Shema, in keeping with the Talmud's dictum, "Once you have declared Him king over (all that is) above and below and the four corners of the heavens, no more is required"* (*Berakhot* 13b).

The virtue of the above interpretation is that it reconciles two divergent tendencies: the philosophical-mystical concept of divinity, which is so rarefied and abstract, so genuinely radical, that it cannot be compared or connected to the material world; and the dialogic nature of divinity expressed in the Torah, which focuses on the personality of God rather than on His existence, on relationship rather than on ontology. Or put another way, the biblical verse of the Shema that denies ontological validity (i.e., "reality") to the rest of the phenomenal world—including human beings—envisions God as beyond personality, beyond relationship; indeed, if God alone is real and all else is but illusion, then the whole notion of "personality" is meaningless. In contrast, the verse *Barukh shem kevod* affirms and validates both human and divine personality; what this perspective loses in the realm of pure unity it gains in the vitality of dynamic relationship.

Strongly opposed to R. Shneur Zalman and R. Ḥayyim's interpretation is the view of the Ziditchover.[5] He faults their acosmic concept as too recondite, too "philosophical"—a term that, in those days and in those circles, was tantamount to a charge of heresy. He is clearly very uncomfortable with the pantheism that is the other side of the coin of acosmism: "there is nothing but God" points the way to "everything is God." Hasidic immanentism (or panentheism)[6] always had to combat this charge of pantheism leveled at it by mitnagdic circles; with this metaphysical debate, it now emerges in intra-hasidic polemics as well.

But one gathers from the Ziditchover's critique that he opposes his colleagues' radical interpretation of divine unity not only because it courts heretical notions of God, but also because it veers too far from ordinary experience to be religiously compelling; indeed, by *denying* ordinary daily experience, it distances the notion of divine Oneness from all but the most sophisticated worshiper. The warmth, the passion, the all-absorbing commitment to God that we ought to feel when reciting the Shema fails to stir within us; instead, we only experience such sentiments when reciting the non-biblical verse, the *Barukh shem kevod.* Thus, even the most learned worshiper is thereby estranged from the Shema itself.

How then does the Ziditchover distinguish between the two terms of the Zohar and the two verses of the Shema? He points to the different *directions* that each of the two verses implies. The biblical verse, he says, points upward, "from below to above"; the traditional verse points to the reverse direction, "from above to below." Of course, "direction" must not be taken literally. In kabbalistic usage, "above" indicates the cause, and "below," the effect. So, when we recite the Shema and proclaim the "Higher Unification," we proceed from below to above, elevating our thoughts from the realm of multiplicity and fragmentation to the pure unity of the First Cause. We ascend mentally from world to world, toward greater oneness, purity, and holiness, from effect to cause, until we attain the highest of the empyrean worlds.

The "Higher Unification" is identified with the Tetragrammaton, the divine Four-Letter Name translated as "the Lord" and conventionally referred to as *Hashem.* This Name represents pure unity and also denotes *kelaliut,* or comprehensiveness. The "Lower Unification" is signified by the Name *Elohim,* "God," and denotes the active principle of the world—representing only a *perat,* or detail, within the comprehensiveness of "the Lord."

Therefore, when we recite the Shema, we encounter the "Higher Unification" of which the Zohar speaks, ascending from *Elohim* to *Hashem,* from "God" to "the Lord," uniting the former with the latter as we ascend from a lowel to a higher level. We move from "below to above," our mind striving to comprehend the utter unity of the divine First Cause, as we affirm a unity in which the dynamic principle of the non-divine realms, the "detail," expressed in the Name *Elohim,* is absorbed into the cosmic comprehensiveness of the Tetragrammaton. We include ourselves along with human souls, with all things living and inanimate, with all the worlds both astronomical and spiritual—in an awesome and loving fellowship of all existence, elevating them with us to the One, the Cause of all causes, "He who is One and not part of counting."[7] In this way the Name *Elohim* is united with the Ineffable Name, the Tetragrammaton, and in their unity they reach to *Eḥad*, the First Cause. This, then, is the expression of the "Higher Unification": the elevation of all worlds to the *Ein Sof*, an ascending spiritual movement driven by the profound yearning[8] of the soul to unite with the *Ein Sof*, a soul ready to abandon all and to sacrifice all for the sake of that union.

As for the "Lower Unification," we reverse direction moving from above to below:

> After we have raised and have ourselves risen to be united with the "One" in truth, then we draw down, by virtue of the unification that pertains to *Barukh shem kevod*, the effluence *(shefa)* of His will, [opening] the channels of the blessing from the One[9] . . . and drawing down His love from its source in the ineffable Name ("the Lord") to this world. . . . This is known as the "Lower Unification," for we draw down the Ancient of Ancients to be with and unite with us here below . . . in the world of *Malkhut* ("kingdom") . . . the Above uniting with the Below.[10]

According to the Ziditchover, when we recite the Shema, we acknowledge that our lives, normally so fragmented and atomized, so disconnected and chaotic—can become integrated, along with all the rest of the created world, only in the unity of the Creator Himself. Thus, in reciting *Barukh shem kevod,* we *pray* that the *shefa*, the divine fullness of relationship, an effluence of sanctity and blessing, flows down from God in His perfect unity, until it unites with us in this World of Fragmentation, the *alma de'peruda.*

Not only does the Ziditchover's meditation help effect divine unification; it also aids in healing the human soul, which is so frequently fractured as a consequence of sin. For sin introduces the element of incoherence into an individual's personality. When I sin, theory and practice, rhetoric and praxis, go in opposite directions. Although I firmly believe one way, I conduct myself otherwise. Sin causes dissonance within me; it disrupts the integrity and rhythm of my character. In sinning, I find myself in opposition to divine Oneness. But the Ziditchover's meditation summons me to restore the unity of my own soul.

For R. Shneur Zalman and R. Ḥayyim, the two first verses of the Shema are complementary, one issuing from the divine and the other from the human perspective and both dealing with the theme of Oneness.[11] For the Ziditchover, they are different thematically: the biblical verse affirms oneness as we elevate ourselves and, along with ourselves, all of creation by reaching out to the holy and pure One; the following verse is a plea, a petition, to that One to open the channels of His love and blessing to those who inhabit His earthly domain. The Ziditchover's interpretation runs no risk of pantheistic deviation, and it is assumed to be "non-philosophical." God's unity remains the primary theme of the Shema; the inserted traditional verse then serves as a prayer *to* God rather than an affirmation *about* Him.[12]

One of the significant corollaries to the theology of R. Shneur Zalman and R. Ḥayyim Volozhiner is the high value placed on *bittul ha-yesh,* the mental nullification of one's very being. The spiritual annihilation of the ego has always been advocated in the quietistic trends of the Kabbalah, which emphasize and value human passivity before God. Such a belief articulates especially well with a theology nullifying all non-divine existence, as in the radical interpretation of the first verse of the Shema.

Both R. Shneur Zalman and R. Ḥayyim were strongly influenced by the Lurianic tradition of Kabbalah that is characterized by a generalized asceticism. While the theme of self-abnegation and a streak of asceticism run throughout much of rabbinic thinking in post-Lurianic generations,[13] this was by no means unanimously accepted. Thus, for example, R. Zadok Hakohen writes:

> Just as a man must believe in God, so must he, afterwards, believe in himself, that is, [he must believe] that God relates to him, that he is not an idle laborer who is here today and gone tomorrow. He must believe that his soul issues from the [divine] Source of all Life, and that God delights in him and derives pleasure from him when he carries out His will.[14]

For R. Zadok, we reach the acme of our spiritual development not by negating our existence but, on the contrary, by affirming our autonomous selfhood as creatures worthy of confronting our Creator and serving Him out of that conviction.

Although other hasidic thinkers as well were opposed to this radical interpretation of the Shema, Ḥabad Hasidism understandably supports this view articulated by its founder, the author of the *Tanya*. Indeed, R. Shneur Zalman's view is sometimes affirmed in hyperbolic, often presumptuous terms, to the point of declaring the opposing view halakhically invalid, even though halakhic judgment on this matter remains ambiguous.[15] But an occasional expression of ideological jingoism should not blind us to the sophistication of R. Shneur Zalman and R. Ḥayyim's interpretation, though it is not easily accessible to minds unaccustomed to thinking dialectically. Their paradoxical explanation of the Zohar's "Higher Unification" and "Lower Unification" is truly admirable.

Yet despite the intellectual appeal of their view, it lacks the emotional satisfaction and spiritual uplift of the Ziditchover interpretation. The latter is *religious* rather than *theological*. To identify ourselves with all the human fraternity and all of creation is a particularly inspiring experience. And as we ascend in our prayer to the absolute One who opens up for us the channels of His relatedness, of His divine blessing and healing, we feel that our broken and incoherent lives are made whole as we join in declaring God's unity. In the divine *yiḥud,* we ourselves become one.[16]

CHAPTER 8

"One" and Contemporary Science

*E*had is an issue not only for theologians and religious lay-men but, in a non-theistic context, for scientists and philosophers as well—in fact, it ultimately concerns all human beings. Indeed, although starting out from totally different vantage points, religious and scientific considerations of unity run parallel; both acknowledge unifying forces in the universe—and perhaps beyond it. In this chapter, we will briefly discuss how the concept of divine unity is refracted through the two lenses of modernity. First, we will consider how contemporary physicists now view the natural universe. Then we will turn to the question of the psycho-cultural orientation of modern society and to its relation to God.

Albert Einstein, after successfully developing his revolutionary theories—the special and the general theories of relativity—next turned his attention to discovering the underlying pattern of the entire universe, seeking a single theory that would embrace all physical phenomena from the cosmic to the subatomic. That ambition to formulate a "theory of everything" has so far proved elusive. Einstein died before he could find the great unified field theory of physics that could account for the four forces of Nature: gravitation, electromagnetism, and both the weak and strong nuclear forces within the atom. That unified theory has still not been discovered. Although proponents of a "super-string" theory have recently made claims for such a unifying concept within their models of the universe, many physicists are skeptical. This quest remains central to legions of nuclear physicists. Like the Jewish monotheistic intuition that one absolutely "simple" Creator is responsible for both the creation and governance of Nature,[1] modern scientists instinctively believe that a fundamental unity underlies all natural phenomena.

However, not all physicists share this conviction that one unified theory can explain or describe all of Nature, that all natural phenomena are somehow reflections of an underlying cosmic unity. Some distinguished scientists, albeit a minority, believe that such an equation or theory will never be found, either because it is undiscoverable or—more significantly—because it simply doesn't exist. In their view, the cosmos is composed of a multiplicity of unrelated forces. There *is* no underlying unity of all creation.

Is it legitimate to draw an analogy between the creation—the physical universe—and the Creator, to assert that the unity of the one truly reflects the unity of the Other? And what of the contrary claim, that Nature is not characterized by an underlying unity? Would proving this claim true deny the unity of the Creator? Or might it do just the reverse?

This controversy is not entirely new. Predating contemporary scientists by almost a thousand years, two of the greatest medieval Jewish philosophers debated the same questions with a similar degree of ardor and sophistication. Saadia (882–942) and Maimonides (1135–1204) both agree that this understanding of the natural universe flows from our affirmation of divine unity.[2] But they hold profoundly different views on what that understanding is.

For Saadia, the unity of God is so exclusive that nothing else can lay claim to this attribute. Thus, the cosmos must necessarily be multiple. Were he alive today, Saadia undoubtedly would side with those physicists who argue *against* a unified field theory. Thus, he writes:

> [Inasmuch as] the Creator of the universe, exalted and magnified be He, is essentially one, it follows by logical necessity that His creatures be composed of many elements, as I have made clear in the foregoing.
>
> At this point, now, I would say that the thing that generally gives the appearance of constituting a unity, whatever sort of unity it be, is singular only in number. Upon careful consideration, however, it is found to be of a multiple nature. To reduce this generalization to simpler terms, when the substances of all beings are analyzed, they are found to be endowed with the attributes of heat and cold and moisture and dryness. When the substance of the tree is examined, it is found to include, in addition to the aforementioned, branches and leaves and fruits, and all that is connected therewith. When the human body, again, is examined, it is found to be composed, besides the elements listed above, of flesh and bones and sinews and arteries and muscles and all that goes with them. This is a matter about which no doubt can be entertained and the reality of which is not to be denied. All these phenomena are in accord with the laws of creation: namely, that the Creator, exalted and magnified be He, be One and His works manifold. That is also borne out by such statements of the Scriptures as, "How manifold are Thy works, O Lord! In wisdom hast Thou made them all" (Ps. 104:24).[3]

Maimonides, contrariwise, draws the exactly opposite conclusion from the identical premises. According to him, the unity of God gives rise not to the world's manifold quality but to its unitary nature. Thus:

Know that the whole of being is one individual and nothing else. I mean to say that the sphere of the outermost heaven with everything that is within it is undoubtedly one individual having in respect of individuality the rank of Zayd and Umar. The differences between its substances, I mean the substances of this sphere with everything that is within it, are like unto the differences between the limbs of a man, for instance. Thus just as Zayd, for instance, is one individual and is at the same time composed of various parts of the body, such as the flesh and the bones and of various mixtures and of several spirits, the sphere in question as a whole is composed of the heavens, the four elements, and what is compounded of the latter. . . .

And Maimonides here goes into a lengthy scientific discourse demonstrating how the physical world, astronomically and biologically, functions as a whole, integrating its various parts. He then continues:

Accordingly, it behooves you to represent to yourself in this fashion the whole of this sphere as one living individual in motion and possessing a soul. For this way of representing the matter to oneself is most necessary or most useful for the demonstration that the deity is one, as shall be made clear. By means of this representation it will also be made clear that the One has created one being.

Maimonides then returns to his analogies from Nature, in order to demonstrate that the world is one by virtue of a single governing principle. Thus he concludes:

In the same way, there exists in the universe a certain force which controls the whole and sets into motion its first and principal parts, granting it the motive power for governing the rest. . . . Without that force, the existence of this sphere and every part of it would be impossible. This force is the Deity, may His name be exalted.[4]

Unlike Saadia, Maimonides sees the entire cosmos as one large organism. Indeed, it is precisely this unitary character of the creation that leads us to conclude that the Creator is One. For Maimonides, this analogy from Nature explains how the One can be the author of the many: the world is not "many" but one; thus, the unity of existence and the unity of the Creator reflect each other. Of course, the character of that natural unity differs from God's unity: the divine unity is simple; the unity of the world, compound—that of an organism rather than that of a "simple" substance.

Most modern scientists reflect the intuition of Maimonides. They seek a grand unified field theory and, in general, prefer "simple" and elegant explanations that will account for all natural forces—gravity, electromagnetism, and the strong and weak atomic forces—under one theoretical roof, despite the fact that no independent scientific evidence has proven the objective superiority of such comprehensive theories over those that provide separate explanations for different sets of phenomena. In contrast, those who argue for diversity in Nature accord with the views of Saadia, for whom the multiplicity of the creation testifies to the unity of the Creator. Thus, the theme of divine unity at the core of the Shema suggests intriguing parallels to the structure of contemporary science.

We now turn our attention from the natural to the human world. How does the idea of unity figure into our sense of ourselves? No longer are we looking at divine unity as it is reflected in mute Nature—either as unified or as diverse—but at divine unity as it shapes our modern sensibilities, our fundamental psychology, our cultural outlook. In other words, we are interested in this unity not as a *fact,* but as a *value* in human life and civilization. In this context, the Saadianic view describes the prevailing anthropological reality, whereas the Maimonidean view represents a vision, a glimmer of a hope.

One contemporary writer, pointing to the contradictory and fragmented quality of modern life, its multiplicity and diversity, concludes that such erosion of our sense of cohesion and unity is inevitable in contemporary society.[5] The more sophisticated we become, the more aware we are of the enormous complexity of nature, of human beings, of the mind, of life in general; the more sensitive we are to the vast variety that abounds in the world, the more do we identify with the trees and not the forest. As William Butler Yeats said in his powerful poem, "The Second Coming":

> Things fall apart; the center cannot hold;
> Mere anarchy is loosed upon the world,
> The blood-dimmed tide is loosed, and everywhere
> The ceremony of innocence is drowned;
> The best lack all conviction, while the worst
> Are full of passionate intensity.

Indeed, we often feel adrift, without a center. The "global village," about which we have heard so much, integrates technology and business, not our lives as individuals. What the late Ludwig Lewisohn complained about American Jewry is true of the rest of the world: we have assimilated not on the level of America's finest thinkers, but on the level of junk literature, mindless television, nihilistic and hedonistic entertainment. As individual men and women, we have succumbed to an "anarchic pluralism" that leads us into a contemporary idolatry in the form of a "sophisticated hedonistic individualism."[6] The Zohar calls such a state the *alma de'peruda*, the "World of Dis-integration" or, in the powerful imagery later introduced by R. Isaac Luria, the "breaking of the vessels," that at the be-

64

ginning of time left the unitary quality of existence shattered. Indeed, social psychologists and philosophers have long characterized human life, particularly modern life, as a state of alienation and estrangement.

In this milieu of incohesiveness and fragmentation, Judaism bids us recite the Shema. If—and this is an important *if*—we assume that the theological unity of God reflects the existential unity of humanity, then we must understand the Shema's message of God as *eḥad* as a beckoning vision, not as a description of current reality. The unity of God is, unquestionably, not yet a fact; it must await, as the Sifre maintained, eschatological fulfillment. But that fulfillment must not be merely a passive one, relegated only to the heart. If not (yet) a fact, it must be championed as a value. It must motivate an active program so that all of life will move toward realizing that "And the Lord shall be king over all the earth"; that the "World of Disintegration" will one day be replaced by the "World of Unity" and reintegration.

The disparity between what is and what ought to be, between fact and value, between "the Lord our God *is* One" and "On that day the Lord *shall* be One and His Name One," implies a certain tension. If we are called upon actively to help realize the future, how can we declare that God is one? Yet that is precisely how these two tendencies produce psychologically conflicting results. If we declare that "God *is* one," implying that humanity is not unified (as Saadia would have it), then we are not summoned to aggressive attempts to implement His unity by actively inviting redemption and promoting the Messianic program. If, however, the divine unity is a value (as Maimonides holds), so that "the Lord *shall* be one," it follows that we have a duty to bring down the Messiah from heaven to earth, as it were. All agree that we believe in the coming of the Messiah; what to do, if anything, to hasten his arrival is where the extrapolations of these two views differ. The former counsels *patience*, the latter *anticipation* as we await redemption.

This is a tension that will never be resolved, not until the coming of the Messiah. It is our fate and destiny to participate in this millennial balancing act, yielding neither to despair nor to the illusion that the "end of history" is at hand.

The challenge of helping to fulfill the divine *yihud* is therefore a very real one, summoning Jews to pursue the vision of *yihud Hashem* on many levels simultaneously. We are called upon to focus our *kavvanah*, our intention, when reciting the Shema; to keep alive and flourishing expectation of the Messianic redemption by creating the proper conditions for it, while at the same time rejecting the allure of pseudo-Messianism in any form or shape; to advance the fortunes of the State of Israel, not only for its own sake but also as a *possible* harbinger of the Messianic era; to ingather the exiles from lands of oppression and from "the four corners of the earth"; to make *aliyah* ourselves; and so on. And all this is to be carried out without impatience and without demanding immediate gratification. For such an impatience has too often led and can again lead to cataclysmic results.

In the opinion of Rabbi Joseph B. Soloveitchik (see also the reference to this in the appendix), the first verse of the Shema fulfills not only the requirement to proclaim the unity of God, but also the mitzvah to love God and to study His Torah. In other words, our love of God and study of Torah must be energized by the grand quest for divine unity. These teachings have special meaning for those who have the good fortune and resolve to devote time regularly to the study of Torah, especially those privileged to study in a community of students and scholars all dedicated to Torah. But they are relevant to all other Jews as well. For our study of the Shema has demonstrated that *talmud torah*, the ongoing and ever deepening study of Torah, is not isolated from the rest of one's existence. On the contrary, it represents the unifying force of life, its existential glue. Torah study must therefore never lead us to a paralyzed introversion, to intellectual, spiritual, or communal self-involvement that constrains our concern for those outside our immediate circle. While mastery of Torah requires periods of retreat from society and mundane affairs—as does mastery of any great discipline—Torah must never be regarded as a self-enclosed system that turns its back on the world. Rather, it is the instrument for unifying the world under the Holy One. Therefore the goal of Torah study must be to unify, to bring coherence to our own lives and, in expanding circles, to our community, to our people, and to all humankind.

Seen from this perspective, the study of Torah becomes more inclusive, comprehending within it the "secular" or worldly disciplines that must be integrated with Torah as part of the drama of unifying the divine Name. Indeed, *Torah Umadda,* the integration of sacred and "secular" studies, is an ideal of *avodat Hashem,* the lifelong service of God. For when we expand the boundaries of Torah study, we discover that it constitutes a "unified field theory," allowing us simultaneously to fulfill the mitzvot of unifying God, loving God, and studying Torah.[7]

Viewed from this "activist" standpoint, *yiḥud Hashem,* as articulated in the first verse of the Shema, becomes not only a holy *concept* but, even more, an extraordinarily powerful *value* that energizes the worshiper to spiritual ambition even without the promise of immediate success.

Perhaps this is one reason that we place our hand over our eyes when reciting the Shema, following the practice of R. Judah the Prince (*Berakhot* 13a). The gesture declares that *yiḥud Hashem* is not only an idea in our head, not only a dream in our mind's eye; it is also a value that governs our conduct, a principle that directs our action, a program that must be carried out by our hands. The hands must do what the eyes envision.

CHAPTER 9

"Blessed Be the Name of His Glorious Kingdom Forever and Ever"[1]: The Interloping Verse

This verse is non-biblical in origin. In chapter 3 we mentioned the Talmud's explanation as to why this verse is recited in an undertone: it was not recited by Moses, but was uttered by Jacob on his deathbed, and therefore we compromise by whispering it.

Three major elements are articulated in this verse:

    a. Praise of the Creator. The Mishnah records that this verse was recited by the congregation after the High Priest, officiating at the Yom Kippur service in the Holy Temple, uttered the Tetragrammaton "in purity and holiness" (*Yoma* 35b).

    b. The Eternity of God. *Barukh shem kevod* is a longer form of the well-known *amen*, indicating assent or belief, except that it is more inclusive in that it comprehends the element of the eternity of God as well. The Mishnah teaches that on the occasion of a public fast, the congregation responds to the blessings uttered by the reader *(ḥazzan)* with the word *amen*. The Gemara limits this practice to a service being conducted outside the Temple; in the Temple itself one must respond with the more elaborate formula, *Barukh shem kevod* (*Taanit* 16b). The Talmud offers as the source of this halakha the verse in Nehemiah (9:5): "Stand up and bless the Lord your God *for ever and ever;* and blessed be Your glorious name which is exalted above all blessing and praise." This verse links God's eternity with the praise of God's Name: *Barukh shem kevod*.

c. The Liturgical Sanctification of the Divine Name *(kiddush Hashem bi'devarim)*. The Halakha teaches that the divine Name is sanctified not only by an act of martyrdom, and not only by exemplary moral conduct, but also by proclaiming faith in God's holiness in public prayer. In all such cases of liturgical *kiddush Hashem,* such as the recitation of the Kaddish, *Kedushah,* or *Barkhu,* the mitzvah is performed in the form of a dialogue: the reader issues the summons to perform the sanctification, and the congregation responds. The verse *Barukh shem kevod* represents such a response to the mention of the divine Name(s) in the Shema.[2]

These three major themes found in *Barukh shem kevod* aptly reflect the first verse of the Shema, which explains why this traditional verse is paired with the biblical verse, the Shema itself. The Shema obviously expresses "praise of the Creator." It also implies God's eternity: the three mentions of divine Names in the Shema refer to God's sovereignty before creation, during the existence of the universe, and after the destruction of all creation.[3] And the Shema and *Barukh shem kevod* are paired as responsive affirmations of the holiness of God, both sanctifying the divine Name.[4]

Given all the above conflicting or at least divergent interpretations, what *kavvanah* ought one entertain while reciting the Shema? From the retort to R. Jeremiah in *Berakhot* 13a (see chapter 6), we learn that the recitation of the Shema should be neither rushed nor dragged out too long so that others are disturbed. In those synagogues where the entire congregation recites the Shema (or at least the first verse) in unison, this problem is exacerbated because the time for the intense mental concentration of *kavvanah* is strictly limited. Does this mean that one should change this custom or avoid such synagogues that may seem too "modern" in their overemphasis on decorousness? While there is much to be said for individual variation even during communal prayer, there are countervailing values that must be considered. Singing—not only reciting—the Shema by the entire congregation in unison is recommended by the Midrash in no uncertain terms:[5]

> "You who dwells in the gardens, the companions hearken to your voice; cause me to hear it. Make haste, my beloved, and be like a roe or a young hart upon the mountains of spices." (Song of Songs 8:13, 14)

> When Jews gather in the synagogues and read the Shema with focused attention, with one voice . . . and with one melody, so that they all conclude [the recitation] together, the Holy One says to them, "You who dwell in the gardens," when you are *companions* (because you read the Shema in unison), I and My [angelic] retinue "hearken to your voice." But when Jews read the Shema in disorder, one earlier and one later, thus not focusing their *kavvanah* in [reciting] the Shema, the Holy Spirit cries out, saying, "Make haste, my beloved, and be like a roe or a young hart"[6]—referring to the supernal hosts who emulate My glory with one voice and with one melody, "upon the mountains of spices"[7]—in the highest of the high heavens.[8]

Any of the various meditations already mentioned is acceptable as an appropriate *kavvanah*. One can, in light of the midrash mentioned earlier,[9] intend to address our Father Jacob and proclaim, to him as it were, that we still do and always will worship the One God who covenanted with him and his children. Indeed, one can even reflect on this while saying the word "Hear O *Israel*" and then refocus one's thoughts on the usual interpretation, namely, that we are repeating Moses' address to his people Israel.

The simplest *kavvanah* is to meditate, when we say "the Lord is our God," on unifying the various dichotomies that cluster about these two Names. This thought should immediately be followed by the eschatological meditation, that is, that this unification is something we Jews now accept wholeheartedly and that the rest of the world will yet accept—at the time of the final redemption.

After these initial meditations, one has a variety of options. One can think of the Talmud's minimalist or comprehensive meditation—that God is omnipresent in space and, perhaps (following Rav Kook), in time as well—even though the Talmud recommended this *kavvanah* only when time is limited. Or, one may focus on the exclusivist interpretation advocated by a number of the Rishonim.

After these meditations have been practiced so that they can be fit into a reasonable time span such as mandated by R. Ḥiyya b. Abba to R. Jeremiah in the Talmud, one can proceed to the complex level of kabbalistic interpretations. Here one can focus one's intention either on R. Shneur Zalman and R. Ḥayyim's acosmic view or on the directional interpretation of the Ziditchover. If one chooses the former, one need not bear in mind the Talmud's meditation, because the acosmic notion transcends that of omnipresence. If the Ziditchover's, it is sufficient in its own right, even though it does not comprehend the Talmud's interpretation. (That, however, should not prove disturbing because, as has been said, the Talmud was concerned only with time constraints, not with the content of the *kavvanah*.)

Obviously, it is not possible to practice all these meditations at one and the same recitation, especially if one is just beginning to prepare for more complex *kavvanot*. It is better to divide the various meditations among the four daily recitations of the Shema.[10] Thus, in the course of the day, one can "cover all bases," thereby guiding one's prayer via the most cogent interpretations of the holiest verse in all of the Torah.

PART II

The Second Verse

CHAPTER 10

Maimonides on
"You Shall Love"[1]

The first word of this verse, *ve'ahavta,* "you shall love" ("the Lord your God with all your heart and all your soul and all your might"), introduces us to one of the fundamental precepts of Judaism: *ahavat Hashem,* the love for God. This powerful theme, central to religion in general and especially to Judaism,[2] has engaged the attention and careful scrutiny of almost every major Jewish thinker. Because a comprehensive history of this concept in Jewish thought is beyond the scope of this volume,[3] I will focus on representative selections from the history of Jewish thought that pertain to our discussion of the Shema and to the interrelationship of spirituality and law in Judaism.

However, before we proceed to more analytic interpretations of our key verse, bearing on the nature of our love for God, let us linger briefly on a midrash that gives an entirely different "spin" to the commandment: "love the Lord your God."

The Sifre understands the verb *ve'ahavta,* "and you shall love," as causative:

> Another explanation of, "You shall love the Lord your God" (Deut. 6:4): *Cause* Him to be beloved by humans, even as your father Abraham did, as it is written, "[And Abram took Sarai his wife, and his brother's son Lot and all the substance that they had gathered] and the souls that

they had gotten in Haran" (Gen. 12:5). (Sifre to Deuteronomy, *pesikta* 32)

"The souls that they had gotten in Haran" is interpreted by
the Sages as referring to the proselytes whom Abraham and
Sarah had converted from paganism to monotheism. Hence, to
love God means to act so as to make Him beloved of others.

In a parallel text in the Talmud, this same theme is recorded
more elaborately:

> Abaye cited a *baraita:* "'You shall love the Lord your God'
> (Deut. 6:4) means that because of you the Name of Heaven
> will become beloved." [This means] that when a person
> studies Scripture and Mishnah and serves scholars of the
> Torah, and he speaks softly with other people, and his deal-
> ings in the market place are proper, and his business is con-
> ducted honestly—what do people say about him? [They
> say:] "Happy is so-and-so who studied Torah; happy is his
> father who taught him Torah; happy is his teacher who
> taught him Torah; woe to those who have not studied
> Torah. Have you seen so-and-so who studied Torah? How
> beautiful are his manners! How refined are his deeds!
> (*Yoma* 86a)

Thus, both the Sifre and the Talmud consider the love of God
as a functional and social as well as a personal and emotional
commandment: we are to live and act so that others (*beriyot*,
literally all human "creatures," whether Jews or non-Jews,
believers or nonbelievers) turn to Him in love. This parallels the
commandment of *kiddush Hashem,* the "sanctification of the
Name," which we discussed earlier (see chapter 5).

To Maimonides, the passages we have just discussed consti-
tuted far more than an engaging homily. In fact, he mentions
them prominently in his work on the commandments, where

they take up fully one-half of his description of the mitzvah of loving God.[4] Let us now turn our attention more directly to what Maimonides has to say about the precept itself: "And you shall love the Lord your God."

Clearly, no serious consideration of Jewish thought or philosophy can omit the views of Maimonides. The *locus classicus* of his views on *ahavat Hashem* is this passage in his immortal legal code, the *Mishneh Torah:*

> What is the way to attain the love and fear of God? When a man contemplates His great and wondrous deeds and creations, and sees in them His unequaled and infinite wisdom, he immediately loves and praises and exalts Him, and is overcome by a great desire to know the great Name; as David said, "My soul thirsts for God, for the living God" (Ps. 42:3). And when he considers these very matters, immediately he withdraws and is frightened and knows that he is but a small, lowly, dark creature who, with his inferior and puny mind, stands before Him who is perfect in His knowledge; as David said, "When I consider Your heavens, the work of Your fingers . . . what is man that You are mindful of him?" (Ps. 8:4, 5). Thus do I explain many great principles concerning the actions of the Master of the Worlds, [namely,] that they provide an opportunity for a wise person to love God. As the Sages said concerning love, "as a result of this you will come to know Him by whose word the world came into being." (*Hilkhot Yesodei ha-Torah,* 2:2)

According to Maimonides, the two religious emotions of love and fear share a common origin: the contemplation of the cosmos. Deep reflection on the creation leads to two apparently divergent religious effects: *ahavat Hashem* (love of God) and *yirat Hashem* (fear of God). Although different, these two emotions are fundamentally linked to each other. We cannot discuss, let alone understand, the one without the other.

Furthermore, love and fear serve as mirror images of each other. Love for God represents a centrifugal motion of the self: overwhelmed by the wisdom we see revealed in the marvels of creation, we seeks to reach outward and upward toward the Creator in order to know Him better. Fear of God is the precise opposite: overwhelmed by the greatness of the Creator, we realize our own triviality, our marginality, and our very nothingness. And so, in a centripetal counter-motion we pull ourselves inward and retreat into ourselves.[5]

Note the implicit relationship between love and fear: our first reaction as we contemplate Nature is, instinctively and impulsively, to feel love. But our reaching out to know the Creator is, intuitively and instinctively, countered and curtailed by the limiting impulse of fear. Maimonides' use of *mi-yad,* which we have translated in its usual sense of "immediately," applied both to love and to fear, fittingly captures this sense of an intuitive reaction, *immediate* because it is unmediated.[6]

Yet, despite the fact that love is immediately constrained by fear, Maimonides obviously agrees with the Sages that "love is greater than fear"—thus, he concludes, the halakha focuses on love alone, explaining that the Creator does certain things in order to grant us the opportunity (or will) to love Him. Thus, fear serves a vital but ancillary role to love: it is love that remains the most significant and valuable religious quality.

Let us return briefly to our first observation, that both love and fear emerge from our contemplating the divine wisdom in God's creation. While Maimonides here points to the creation or Nature as the focus of our contemplation in order to arrive at love, he elsewhere includes more than the cosmos as the object of such contemplation. Thus, in *Hilkhot Teshuvah,* 10:6, he presents his severely rationalistic view of the love for God, declaring our love to be proportional to our *knowledge* of Him: "One loves the Holy One only with the mind, thus knowing Him; for love is in accordance with knowledge, whether little or much." He then advises his reader to immerse himself intellectually in the various branches of wisdom that lead to knowing God (and, thus, to loving Him):

> Therefore must a man set aside [time] to understand and comprehend the [various branches of] wisdom and learning that impart to him knowledge of his Creator, depending on man's capacity to understand and apprehend, etc.

The branches of "wisdom and learning" are not necessarily limited to the natural sciences, although they certainly include them. According to Maimonides, our responses to nature must lead us to and be shaped by proper and correct philosophical speculation.

In his work on the commandments, he broadens the canvas even further: "for He has commanded us to love Him; and that [means] to understand and comprehend His mitzvot and His actions."[7] Here Maimonides includes not only God's actions—which may well embrace the divine guidance of history as well as His governance of nature—but also "His mitzvot," His commandments. Maimonides may here be referring indirectly to the study of Torah, repository of the commandments, as a source of inspiration to love God. Writing in his own name, the author of *Sefer ha-Ḥinukh,* who follows Maimonides, states: "That is, along with reflection in Torah necessarily comes a strengthening of love in the heart."[8]

To confirm our interpretation that Maimonides did indeed regard study of Torah as a vital source of *ahavat Hashem,* and not merely an afterthought to his major argument, we need only read further in the same passage, where he cites a proof-text from the Sifre. Maimonides writes, following the aforementioned:

> This is the text of the Sifre: It is said, "You shall love the Lord your God" (Deut. 6:4). But [from this] I do not know *how* one loves Him; therefore is it said, "And these words which I command you this day shall be in your heart" (ibid. 6:6)—as a result of this you will come to know Him by whose word the world came into being.[9]

The antecedent of "as a result of this" is obviously "these words"; this undoubtedly refers to the words of Torah (or, at the very least, the words of the Shema), not to the contemplation of Nature.

However, we still face a dilemma in the interpretation of Maimonides' thought. Is Nature, the divine creation of the cosmos, the sole object whose contemplation leads to the love and fear of God—or is the Torah, the direct revelation of the divine Will, equally a source of such love and fear? In the two passages from his legal code, the *Mishneh Torah,* the first from *Hilkhot Yesodei ha-Torah* ("Laws of the Foundations of the Torah") and the second from *Hilkhot Teshuvah* ("Laws of Repentance"), he clearly stipulates that Nature is the source that inspires us to love and fear God. Yet in *Sefer·ha-Mitzvot,* his work on the commandments, he identifies that inspirational source both as the commandments (using two synonyms) and as His works, i.e., Nature. Thus, in the *Mishneh Torah* he mentions only Nature as the source of the two fundamental religious emotions, whereas in *Sefer ha-Mitzvot* ("Book of the Commandments") he points to both Torah and Nature, emphasizing the former.[10]

Which, then, does Maimonides consider the primary object whose contemplation leads to love: Nature (and, by extension, philosophy, which elaborates upon our love and fear inspired by Nature) or Torah and mitzvot? Is there perhaps a double focus, each holding equal value? Is *Sefer ha-Ḥinukh* offering a valid interpretation of Maimonides' view, or is he imposing his own—and apologetic—view?

We now turn to Maimonides' major philosophical work, the *Guide for the Perplexed*. Here, our guide Maimonides identifies the cosmos as the source of the intuition and subsequent philosophizing that leads us to love and fear. The two most important passages in the *Guide* appear in part III. In chapter 28 of this section, he explains that the Torah, "in regard to the correct opinions through which the ultimate perfection may be attained"—ideas such as God's existence, unity, and power—speaks only in general and apodictic terms, without going into much detail:

> With regard to all the other correct opinions concerning the whole of being . . . the Torah, albeit it does not . . . direct attention toward them in detail . . . does so in summary fashion by saying, "To love the Lord" (Deut. 11:13). You know how this is confirmed in the dictum regarding love: "With all your heart and with all your soul and with all your might" (Deut. 6:5). We have already explained in the *Mishneh Torah* that this love becomes valid only through the apprehension of the whole of being as it is and through the consideration of His wisdom as it is manifested in it.

Here, then, Maimonides points to Nature, its study and philosophical interpretation, as the source of love—as he did in the various passages in the *Mishneh Torah*.

In chapter 52 of part III of the *Guide*, Maimonides distinguishes between two categories of commandments: the practical ones, the do's and the don'ts of scriptural legislation; and the "opinions" or theological propositions taught by the Torah. The former lead to fear of God, the latter to love.

> As for the opinions the Torah teaches us—namely, the apprehension of His being and His unity, may He be exalted—these opinions teach us love, as we have explained several times. You know to what extent the Torah lays stress upon love: "With all your heart," etc. For these two ends, namely, love and fear, are achieved through two things: love through opinions taught by the Torah, which include apprehension of His being as He is in truth; while fear is achieved by means of all actions prescribed by the Torah, as we have explained.

Thus, the *Mishneh Torah* and the *Guide for the Perplexed* assert that Nature and the correct philosophical ideas resulting from its contemplation serve as the source of our love for God, while *Sefer ha-Mitzvot* includes, and appears to emphasize, Torah and the commandments. Is this a trivial inconsistency, or is there something behind Maimonides' apparent contradictions that reconciles and resolves them? I believe that the latter is the case. The principle operating here is one that characterizes much of Maimonides' thought, namely, the distinction between ordinary people and the learned elite.[11]

The average man or woman is expected to observe all the actional commandments—the Halakha—in all their details. Performing these prescribed actions, in addition to comprehending the otherwise profound philosophical ideas concerning God presented in a simple manner by the Torah, is enough to give this average person the wherewithal to conduct his or her life in an orderly, moral, and civilized manner and with an awareness of the basic ideas that characterize Judaism. The mitzvot will guide such a person onto the right path, consistent with his or her intellectual capacity. The elite, however, whose curiosity and intellectual ability raise them above the rest of their peers, are expected to strive for a far higher standard, beyond the limits set by the Torah for the others. Indeed, such a person must aspire to understand the most refined conceptions of the Deity and His attributes.[12]

In *Sefer ha-Mitzvot*, which—as its very name indicates—deals with an enumeration of the commandments, Maimonides is writing for "ordinary" Jews who wish to observe what is required of them and what is within their ability to understand. The very mitzvot that connect such people to the service of God—the behavioral commandments together with the Torah's summary of God's major attributes—constitute the source of their love for God. And to the extent that their ability permits, they may also draw inspiration from Nature and its reflection of the imponderable wisdom of the Creator.[13] But their primary source for religious inspiration remains—the commandments and, of course, the Torah of which they form a part.

However, the *Mishneh Torah* seems to contradict our thesis. As Maimonides' principal halakhic work, it is meant for all Jews equally. Hence here he ought to restrict his discussion of the source of love solely to Torah and mitzvot, omitting the contemplation of the cosmos, which requires a capacity for metaphysical speculation. Yet in two places in this work that Maimonides does discuss love and fear, the context suggests that he is addressing only an elite segment of the people, not all of them.

And so, in the "Laws of the Foundations of the Torah," although his stated goal is to impart, in non-technical terms and in a manner accessible to the layman, the theological foundations of Judaism, we see that the subject matter, though simplified for the masses, remains intrinsically so difficult and so conceptually demanding that even in its simplified form it constitutes a formidable intellectual challenge. Maimonides acknowledges this fact when he maintains that this material is a key to understanding the divine governance of the universe[14] and that it forms the essential content of the *maaseh mer-kavah*—the exegesis of Ezekiel's vision of the divine chariot, which the Sages declared an esoteric study,[15] in contrast to halakhic discourse, which they deemed accessible to all, "young and old, men and women."[16] It is therefore logical that Maimonides identifies the contemplation of Nature as inspiring the intuition that leads to both love and fear. Indeed, since the context of these first chapters of the "Laws of the Foundations of the Torah" concerns matters scientific and metaphysical, it stands to reason that Maimonides focuses here on Nature as the source of love and fear of God rather than the commandments and the Torah.[17]

Now let us turn to a passage in *Hilkhot Teshuvah*, the "Laws of Repentance," where the context shows that Maimonides is here using an alternative definition of fear—the conventional as opposed to his more sophisticated version as presented at the beginning of the "Laws of the Foundations of the Torah." Chapter 10 of the "Laws of Repentance" is devoted to the distinction between those who observe the law for its own sake and those who do so for ulterior motives—such as the desire for reward or the fear of punishment. The latter—which includes "the ignorant, women, and children"—act out of fear, which, of course, is a lower form of religious devotion, whereas the former do so out of love:

> What is the proper kind of love?—when one loves God with very powerful, great, and overflowing love such that his soul is bound up in the love for God, and he finds himself constantly thinking about it as if he were love-sick [for a woman] such that his mind is never distracted from loving and thinking about her constantly, whether sitting or standing, whether eating or drinking. (*Hilkhot Teshuvah*, 10:3)

It is well known that the love for the Holy One does not become bound up with the heart of man until he thinks about it constantly and properly and abandons everything in the world except for it; as we were commanded, "with all your heart and with all your soul." One loves the Holy One only with the mind, thus knowing Him; for love is in accordance with knowledge: if little [knowledge] then little [love], if much [knowledge] then much [love]. Therefore must a person dedicate himself to understand and comprehend the [branches of] wisdom and learning that inform him about his Creator according to his capacity to understand and attain. (Ibid., 10:6)

This form of love goes beyond fear as the latter was described in the "Laws of the Foundations of the Torah"; it operates on a higher level—and, thus, only comes to a person who is prepared "to understand and comprehend the [branches] of wisdom and learning," Maimonides' terms for natural science and metaphysical thinking.

And, of course, in the *Guide,* his often esoteric philosophical *magnum opus,* we expect to find a description of a higher standard intended for the elite, which we most certainly do. So the apparent contradiction within Maimonides' thought dissolves under close scrutiny.

Maharal on "You Shall Love"

R abbi Judah Loew of Prague (CA. 1512–1609), popularly known by his acronym, Maharal, was a singular fountainhead of Jewish ideas. He influenced many of the most important Jewish thinkers of succeeding generations, perhaps most especially those associated with Hasidism, beginning in the last half of the eighteenth century. Indeed, his seminal thought had a profound influence on a number of Jewish religious thinkers in the twentieth century as well. We should therefore not be surprised that he brings original insights to the question of *ahavat Hashem,* the love for God.

We find a number of different definitions and interpretations of this idea in various places in the Maharal's prodigious work. In one passage he draws a well-known distinction between love and fear, namely, that love motivates us to observe the positive commandments, whereas fear restrains us from transgressing the negative commandments[1]—essentially a restatement of Nahmanides' famous distinction between the two.[2]

Elsewhere, he delineates two types of fear: one that is independent of love, and the other—the more common—that is but the disguised face of love and therefore only another facet of our love of God:

> The major part of fear derives from love, for one who loves
> another strives to fulfill his wishes in every possible way, so
> that the love will be indivisible. He therefore fears to vio-
> late [his beloved's] will even in small matters, for that

would negate his love. That is why it is said of Abraham, "for now I know that you are a God-fearing man" (Gen. 22:12).[3]

The Maharal considers this second type of fear, which derives from love, superior to that which is independent of love.[4]

What is most significant and novel in the Maharal's interpretation of *ahavat Hashem* is his version of the acosmic idea of God, which seems to anticipate, by about two centuries, that developed more elaborately by R. Shneur Zalman and R. Ḥayyim.[5] He writes:

> The love of man for God that issues from man alone is of no account. For man comes from God, and man returns to Him, just as everything must return to Him. There is nothing other than God; He is one, and there is nothing else. . . .
>
> From this point of view we can understand love. This is why it is said, "the Lord is our God, the Lord is one" (and immediately thereafter) "You shall love the Lord your God" etc. (Deut. 6:4, 5). Because He is one, there is nothing in existence in the world that is separate from Him, for all depends upon and is attached to Him, for He is the foundation of all. And that is why love is relevant to God.[6]

This interpretation is consistent with the Maharal's general thinking, for he often writes of the longing of the effect to return to its Cause.

Despite the humanistic bent of the Maharal, which has been much commented upon in recent years, he here discounts the "natural" human religious urge. He dismisses the love for God that emerges from within us, the innate part of the natural life of man as *Homo religiosis,* as "of no account." Rather, our spiritual dimension, expressed in our love of God, can be attributed only to the bond of shared reality that ties us to our Creator, the Source of all existence. Only in this metaphysical sense of our ontological indebtedness to God, and in this sense alone, can we be defined as naturally religious beings. The religion we practice to satisfy a psychological need is inferior to the religion that derives from our awareness of humanity's nothingness without God as the core of existence itself. According to this interpretation, we can now understand the sequence in our passage. The Shema's proclamation of divine unity leads directly to the commandment to love God. *Yiḥud Hashem* implies *ahavat Hashem*.

Yet here a question naturally arises: given the infinite distance and dissimilarity between God and human beings, how can we be commanded to *love* God? Indeed, says the Maharal, we are commanded to fear and honor but never to love father, mother, or teacher. The reason is self-evident: love is only possible between equals or near-equals, not between those who are essentially unequal. How, then, is it at all possible to speak of loving God?

Paradoxically, it is the very abyss that separates God and humanity that makes love possible:

> But according to what we have said, there is no difficulty. For although He is in heaven and you are on earth, and the distance between God and man is so great as to defy articulation, the explanation [of the love between them] is . . . that God is the very existence of man, and it is impossible [for man to exist] without Him, and *therefore* is it relevant to speak of loving Him. For everything loves that which is his completion, and God is the completion of man.[7]

For the Maharal, the term *ahavah*, "love," is qualitatively different when applied to God than when applied to humans. Love between humans, no matter how intense, does not require that they dissolve their egos and negate their very existence. But our love for God demands that we recognize the "necessary" or absolute existence of God as opposed to our merely "contingent" existence. The fact that we owe our very existence to God makes our love for God that much more powerful and significant.

The Maharal makes this point quite cogently by referring to the well-known talmudic tale of the martyrdom of R. Akiva. The Talmud (*Berakhot* 61b) relates that when the Romans condemned R. Akiva to death, skinning him alive with metal combs, it was at the time of day that one was required to recite the Shema. As R. Akiva was doing so, his students asked, "Must one indeed go so far (in suffering martyrdom for the sake of God)?" "Indeed so," the master replied, "for all my life I waited for this opportunity (to fulfill the mitzvah of martyrdom); shall I then refrain from so doing now that the opportunity is at hand?" He then recited the Shema, elongating the word *eḥad* (the Lord is *one*) and then expired.

> Now I ask you, how did he fulfill the commandment to love God with all his heart and all his soul by lengthening his recitation of *eḥad* until he expired? The answer is this: Man's love for God that issues from man himself is of no account, for man comes from God and to Him he returns. All returns to God, and nothing [truly] exists other than God, for He is One and naught else [exists]. . . . When [R. Akiva] said, "the Lord is One," implying that nothing else [truly] exists, and thus all that is [ultimately] returns to Him . . . his soul returned completely to God in that He is one; and from this vantage does love exist. That is why it says, "[Hear O Israel] the Lord is our God, the Lord is one, and you shall love the Lord your God," etc.[8]

Here the Maharal reiterates the incommensurability of love for man and love for God and then concludes his homily on R. Akiva:

> Complete love [for God] is that love in which man returns his spirit and his soul to Him completely to the point that man no longer possesses existence, for he is then in total communion with Him. . . . And as R. Akiva said . . . For this is complete love: when he offers up his soul to God (i.e., in martyrdom), for then he is in utter communion (*devekut,* attachment) with Him. This is the essence of love. Thus, we have explained that love appertains more to the love for God (than for a fellow human), in that man offers his life for God and is completely attached to Him. This is true love.[9]

Therefore, when we express *ahavat Hashem* in the Shema, we obligate ourselves to abjure all superficiality and spiritual pettiness and come prepared to offer our lives to Him who is our Source; this is, after all, what the Sages meant when they said, "'with all your soul' (Deut. 6:5)—even if He takes your soul," a theme to which we will return in greater length in chapter 16.

Finally, the Maharal adds another, rather practical dimension to the commandment of *ahavat Hashem,* one that is less overwhelming in its demand upon us: our attitudes toward our fellows—or, better, toward some of them. The Torah commands us to choose the way of life and blessing, "that you may love the Lord your God, and that . . . you may cleave unto Him" (Deut. 30:20). The Talmud comments: Is it possible for a mere human being to "cleave" to God, who is described elsewhere in the Torah as a "consuming fire"? The Sages reply: what Scripture means is that whoever marries his daughter to a Torah scholar or takes care of a scholar's business or in any way provides for a scholar's needs from his own resources, the

Torah considers it as if he had cleaved to the *Shekhinah* itself, the very Divine Presence. Thus, according to the Talmud, we can take an indirect route in order to "cleave" to God, that is, we can cleave to those who spend their lives studying His Torah.

In commenting upon this biblical verse, the Maharal shifts the focus to the first part of the verse, the command to "love" God. How may those of us less endowed with religious fervor or metaphysical yearning or spiritual prowess express our love for God? The Maharal answers: by loving His scholars, those who devote their time and intellects to knowing, analyzing, and teaching His precepts. The Maharal's interpretation thus enables "ordinary" people to participate in spirituality, in fulfillment of the halakhic requirement to love God.

CHAPTER 12

R. Shneur Zalman on "You Shall Love"

The most sophisticated and complex classification of the various forms of *ahavat Hashem,* a kind of morphology of love, is given to us by the Hasidic master, R. Shneur Zalman (1747–1812), both in his *Tanya* and in various other works of his. Building on the solid foundation laid down by his predecessors, especially the (talmudic) Rishonim and the Kabbalists, R. Shneur Zalman reinforces their insight that the love of God requires a high degree of selflessness and that this love must be without any ulterior motive whatsoever (a concept that in the Western world is known by the Greek name, *agape,* as differentiated from *philia,* the love of friends for each other, and *eros,* sexual or erotic love). Like these earlier sages, he judges this love according to its efficacy in leading each of us to refine our character in our interpersonal relations as we strive thereby to please the Creator. R. Shneur Zalman's major contribution to this evolving idea is his exceedingly subtle appreciation for the psychological dimensions of the Jewish religious experience (for that is essentially what *ahavat Hashem* is) and his sensitive categorization of the different types of love of God.[1]

As we have already learned from Maimonides and the Maharal, love and fear go hand in hand; we cannot discuss the one without the other. The Kabbalists were even more outspoken on this matter. The Zohar refers to love and fear as the "two wings" of religious experience.[2] So, for R. Shneur

Zalman, true worship, *avodat Hashem,* is impossible without the expression of these two fundamental sentiments, for just as a bird cannot fly with only one wing, so authentic religious experience depends upon the twin attitudes of love and fear.

R. Shneur Zalman's analysis of love follows upon his analysis of fear. (Since that is not our theme here, we shall touch on the latter only insofar as it enhances our understanding of how he interprets *ahavat Hashem.*) R. Shneur Zalman divides fear into two categories: "Natural Fear" and "Rational Fear." Similarly, he speaks of Natural Love and Rational (or intellectual) Love. Natural Love is also called Hidden Love—*ahavah tiv'it u-mesuteret.* This way of loving God emerges naturally and spontaneously from the depths of our being. In contrast, Rational Love, *ahavah sikhlit,* arises in response to contemplation.

The best way to understand R. Shneur Zalman's theory of Natural Love is to consider it in the context of a compelling question that has troubled many halakhists through the centuries: the matter of *minyan ha-mitzvot,* the numbering of the commandments, about which there is a considerable literature. According to a tradition recorded in the Talmud, the total number is 613. But what is the proper method to determine which of the many commandments in the Torah are to be included and which excluded? All who have written on this theme include loving God as a full commandment. But can the will and the emotions be "commanded"? Can anyone order you when and how and whom to love if you do not feel it in your heart?

R. Shneur Zalman's answer emerges from his understanding of how we love God. We are not commanded to impose upon ourselves an extraneous, extra-human sentiment; rather, this love for God already exists in potential form (and is thus, both "natural" and "hidden") within our soul. The mitzvah to love God demands that we remove all obstacles and impediments that interfere with our free and open expression of that love. In other words, the religious dimension is indigenous to human beings. Each of us is a naturally religious being, a *Homo religiosis*. But this spiritual gift remains latent, undeveloped and unexpressed, unless we carefully nurture this particular "talent."

Although R. Shneur Zalman ascribes little value to qualities that are merely natural, including "Natural Fear," he changes his stance when he deals with "Natural Love." Because the love for God is so refined a quality, so utterly selfless in its genuine form, he finds special value in *ahavah tiv'it u-mesuteret;* indeed, in some ways he considers it superior to Rational Love, *ahavah sikhlit*. Whereas the former is totally non-egotistical, the latter often proves less altruistic. Pure Natural Love requires self-abnegation and self-annihilation—that is, the extinction of the ego. When we love God in this way, we empty ourselves of all wills other than the will to be with and obey our Creator, and this love therefore is "beyond the knowledge of the perceived and the understood." The resulting bonding with God is extremely powerful: indeed, says R. Shneur Zalman, "this love is so wondrous that the soul cannot bear its apperception." This supra-rational love may be compared to the love a child has for his father: The child has no intellectual appreciation of his father's qualities, of his indebtedness to his father, or even of how this man came to be his father. He knows only that he loves this man and longs to be with him. Such is the nature of "Natural and Hidden Love": every Jew possesses this love and yearning of a child for its parent as an integral and natural part of his divine soul, his special psyche.

R. Shneur Zalman also compares *ahavah tiv'it u-mesuteret* to a flame: just as the flame of a candle naturally tends upward, seeking, as it were, to escape from its bondage to the wick and soar heavenward, so too the soul yearns to escape from its enslavement to the body, to return and be reabsorbed in its primal Source, even though it may in the process lose its identity and its separate existence.

But how can this special love be regarded as "natural" when ordinary experience presents us with so many Jews who are remote from Torah and apparently lack all connection with religious feelings? R. Shneur Zalman answers that *ahavah tiv'it u-mesuteret* is "hidden" within all Israel—even within the most crass and vulgar, the most disobedient and rebellious, the most secular and cynical. *Ahavah tiv'it u-mesuteret* in the heart of the non-religious is merely "asleep" or passive; it does not reveal itself in the normal course of everyday life. But when a crisis arises in which a Jew's faith is tested, such as religious persecution by anti-Semites, the "Hidden Love" is aroused from its slumber. At that moment, as history has taught us, even the most obtuse, insensitive, and indifferent Jew is ready to submit to martyrdom and perform *kiddush Hashem*, the sanctification of God's Name. It is crisis, R. Shneur Zalman teaches, that brings out the innate but latent spiritual dimension of the Jew.

Rational Love is an altogether different expression of *ahavat Hashem*, for it contains an egotistical element, albeit of the most subtle and refined kind. Having concluded by means of rational insight or long contemplation that God is the eternal Source of our very existence and the repository of all that is good, we seek to identify and cleave to that divine Source. Therefore, this *ahavah sikhlit* in some measure reflects our self-love or self-concern. In this sense, it is inferior to *ahavah tiv'it u-mesuteret*. Even when we experience the Rational Love that arises from our *gratitude* for all that we owe to our Creator for our very life, we are caught up in a net of self-love. Such gratitude is undoubtedly a virtue, but it is nonetheless not quite as selfless and therefore not quite as noble as totally selfless Natural Love.

Furthermore, *ahavah tiv'it u-mesuteret* is superior to *ahavah sikhlit* because it is constant, whereas Rational Love is present only when the mind actively focuses on the greatness of God. However, when the mind is preoccupied—as inevitably it must be—with other, more prosaic matters, Rational Love is inactive. Such is not the case with natural and hidden love, whose source is in our soul—today we would say, our "unconscious." This love is always with us, independent of conscious mental processes.

R. Shneur Zalman now turns to the other side of the ledger and presents us, in many of his works, with the superior qualities of *ahavah sikhlit*. For one thing, Rational Love is *shaveh le'khol nefesh,* uniformly available to all Jews, no matter what their native dispositions. Even those whose indigenous spiritual capacity is limited can bring themselves, via intellectual contemplation (each on his own level, of course), to *ahavat Hashem.* Not so with *ahavah tiv'it u-mesuteret,* which, although "natural," is also "hidden" and therefore accessible only to the spiritual elite in whom the love has emerged from obscurity into full consciousness. And here we encounter a paradox: this natural but deeply concealed love can be revealed only by means of contemplation; thus, Rational Love becomes the means for attaining Natural and Hidden Love and, because it is indispensable to it, is therefore superior to it. In other words, though religion is natural, the *consciousness* of our religious yearnings is not; it requires a special measure of wisdom and self-awareness to appreciate both the presence of spiritual strivings within ourselves and their universality.

Moreover, this spiritual triumph of self-awareness is an either-or condition, not a matter of degree or level. Not so with cognitive abilities, possessed in common by all humanity. All humans are aware of their ability to reason, even though the quality or level of such ability varies considerably from individual to individual. It is through this universal faculty of reason that we discover and manifest our instinctive spiritual capacities.

Further, the *ahavah sikhlit,* because it is intellectual, has the potential to grow. The more intense our mental effort, the greater will be our love of God. *Ahavah tiv'it u-mesuteret,* however, because it is *natural,* is circumscribed by its very naturalness: it cannot exceed the limits of its preexistence in the soul. It is a *fact, a given.* It cannot expand beyond its outer limit even with effort.

It is for this reason that we must never be satisfied with the degree of love we feel for God, but must combine *ahavah sikhlit* with *ahavah tiv'it u-mesuteret.* On the one hand, our emotional expression of religious experience is inadequate without an intellectual component; on the other hand, even when Rational Love has, by means of contemplation, revealed to us our innate natural and hidden love, we must bear in mind that the ultimate source of that religious experience is not the fruit of intellect alone but issues from a Source that transcends it. After all is said and done, religion springs from God, not man.[3]

Often R. Shneur Zalman uses two other terms for the love of God, which make for some confusion. The first, *ahavah rabbah* (literally, "great love") more or less corresponds to *ahavah tiv'it u-mesuteret;* the second, *ahavat olam* (literally, "eternal love"), to *ahavah sikhlit. Ahavah rabbah* originates from beyond the "worlds," i.e., it is mysterious in its origin, as is the "naturalness" of *ahavah tiv'it u-mesuteret. Ahavat olam,* in contrast, results from meditation upon the "world" *(olam)* or "worlds," which reveal the greatness of the Creator.[4] These two pairs of terms encompass between them the commandment to love God.

CHAPTER 13

R. Zadok Hakohen of Lublin on "You Shall Love"

Zadok Hakohen, who passed away at the dawn of the twentieth century, is only now being "discovered" as a master of creative, original Jewish, especially hasidic, thought. A man of spiritual gifts and a solid halakhic scholar as well, he left behind various works that sparkle with insight and wisdom. Although R. Zadok's development of the theme of love of God is less systematic than R. Shneur Zalman's, his novel comments are exceedingly illuminating and deserve our attention and reflection. In particular, let us focus on two such insights.

Using a different terminology from that of R. Shneur Zalman and a different set of definitions, R. Zadok identifies three kinds of love: *ahavat olam* and *ahavah rabbah,* both discussed in the previous chapter according to R. Shneur Zalman, and *ahavah zuta,* literally, "minor love," derived from a passage in the Zohar (II, 244). *Ahavat olam* and *ahavah rabbah* complement each other, referring to Israel's love for God and God's reciprocal love for Israel. *Ahavah zuta,* in contrast, is unidirectional and refers exclusively to Israel's or humanity's love for God.[1] R. Zadok's *ahavah zuta* parallels the *Tanya's ahavah tiv'it u-mesuteret,* "Natural and Hidden Love." Unlike *ahavah rabbah,* which bursts into consciousness with a consuming passion, this "Minor Love" lies concealed within the human heart as a natural property.

Ahavah rabbah is clearly superior to *ahavah zuta,* just as "Revealed Fear," *yirah be'hitgalut,* is superior to fear hidden in the heart. Drawing upon the verse in Proverbs 27:5, "Open rebuke is better than secret love *(ahavah mesuteret),*" R. Zadok identifies "open rebuke" as "Revealed Fear," which is superior even to "Hidden Love," despite the accepted teaching that "love is greater than fear." However, while we can elevate our "hidden" fear of God from its state of concealment or mere potentiality to a state of revelation (i.e., to awareness in our own consciousness) by external means—in this case, "open rebuke"—we cannot do the same with our hidden love: *ahavah rabbah* remains a gift of God, and without such grace no amount of effort can raise the *ahavah zuta* to the level of *ahavah rabbah.* Here R. Zadok diverges from R. Shneur Zalman, who held that intellectual contemplation can in fact stir the embers of "Natural and Hidden Love" into open and flaming love. According to R. Zadok, both *ahavah zuta* and *ahavah rabbah* are divine gifts, beyond our own manipulation.

R. Zadok tempers this categorization with a legitimate caveat: these distinctions should not be too tightly drawn because spiritual emotions often include one another and over-lap. Although it may be easy for us to analyze and define such ideas philosophically, representing our own religious experi-ence is not so simple. In actual religious life, R. Zadok realisti-cally concedes, the various forms of love and fear coexist; the distinctions we make when we talk about them are more intel-lectual than practical, referring mostly to matters of emphasis.

Historically and typologically, Abraham possessed and sym-bolized *ahavah rabbah.* Isaac, in turn, symbolized fear in its highest, revelatory form, that which is in our hands to create by ourselves, for, as the Talmud teaches, "all is in the hands of Heaven, save the fear of Heaven" (*Berakhot* 33b). However, though his fear was revealed, his love was concealed, in the form of *ahavah zuta*. Lastly, Jacob—often referred to as "the choicest of the Patriarchs"—represented *ahavat olam*, a love that endures under all circumstances.

Of these three spiritual states, *ahavat olam* is the greatest. For *ahavah rabbah*, significant as it is, is ephemeral—although it passionately bursts into brilliant flame, it soon dies down, as does a flame—but *ahavat olam* is more like a banked fire that keeps on burning steadily, offering light and heat. *Ahavat olam* serves "both in good times and bad," which is why (according to the standard prayer book adopted by the Hasidim, known as *nusaḥ Sefarad*), the evening Shema is introduced by *ahavat olam*: As we enter night, the symbol of danger, violence, and foreboding, the *ahavat olam* of Jacob endures.[2] It is only in the morning, as day dawns upon us with promise, that we can speak of *ahavah rabbah*—a sublime experience virtually impossible to attain during the dark night of suffering. Indeed, teaches R. Zadok, since the destruction of the Temple—and the beginning of our long night of exile—*ahavah rabbah* has not been accessible to Israel; only at the Redemption will it reappear and be available again. It is a form of religious experience that has been lost to us and that will return to us at a much later period.

A second passage by R. Zadok in the same work[3] focuses on the various kinds of human love, only one of which is the love for God (analyzed in the previous passage). R. Zadok identifies three kinds of love that humans experience: the love for God, the love of Torah, and the love of Israel.

Our love for God is the source, albeit "concealed," of the other two loves. For without it, our love for Israel—that is, for our fellow Jews—is merely a social phenomenon, our natural craving for human community or ethnic fellowship with no redeeming transcendent dimension. And our love for Torah without an accompanying love for God is merely a quest to satisfy our intellectual curiosity and is devoid of any true spiritual content.

Scriptural history provides graphic illustrations of these forms of deep but imperfect attachment. The Generation of the Flood (Gen. 7:1–8:7)—whose wickedness brought upon the world the deluge that wiped out all life except Noah and his ark-borne menagerie—knew no "love of Israel";[4] there was mutual enmity aplenty. Their utter wickedness reveals neither love of God nor love of man. However, R. Zadok discovers in the Zohar (III, 216b) a source that speaks of their "love of Torah." The reference is not to Torah as such, which had not yet been revealed; rather, "Torah" here symbolizes a love of knowledge and learning. Indeed, so enamored were they of the search for wisdom, the Zohar teaches, that this generation would have been worthy to receive the Torah, were it not for their total lack of obedience to and love for God. It was this lack of faith that led them, despite their intellectual superiority, to widespread debauchery and ultimately to destruction.

The Generation of the Tower (Gen. 11:1–9)—who, after the Flood, attempted to build a skyscraper to reach Heaven—experienced "love of Israel," i.e., human fellowship and communal solidarity, but no love of God; indeed, their intent was to dethrone God. Their punishment fit their crime: since their love for each other was hollow at its core, God "confounded their language" so that they could not communicate with each other and "scattered them from thence upon the face of all the earth," thus undoing their community altogether. Social cohesiveness and mutual responsibility are inadequate without a religious anchor.

The Children of Israel, however, as "the seed of Abraham," have implanted in them—genetically, as it were—the love for God. (This idea recalls R. Shneur Zalman's assertion that Jews exemplify all human beings who are innately religious.) This love expresses the *sefirah* of *Keter*, "Crown," the highest of the ten *sefirot*, the unfolding self-revelation of the *Ein Sof*—the Infinite One God who, in His self-contained essence, is beyond all characterization. *Keter*, which stands above the *sefirot* of *Ḥokhmah* and *Binah*, "Wisdom" and "Understanding," is, by virtue of this priority and its closeness to the *Ein Sof*, mysterious and beyond reason. This supreme love is the source that vitalizes, for the Jew, the other two loves—the love of Torah, which is parallel to Wisdom, and the love of Israel, parallel to Understanding. As in the classical sefirotic structure, Wisdom and Understanding derive their vitality and very existence from (the *Ein Sof* via) the Crown. Indeed, the love for God is unmovable and unassailable; it is beyond intellect, functioning in the realm of faith at its most mysterious and sublime, and cannot be destroyed even by sin itself: as the Talmud teaches, "an Israelite, even if he sins, remains an Israelite" (*Berakhot* 6b). Hence, only by means of *ahavat Hashem*, love for God, can we attain the other two loves in an enduring and pure manner.

Thus we reach an interesting conclusion: that our love of God naturally leads us to love of Israel and love of Torah. We find this proposition affirmed in the verse following the commandment, "You shall love the Lord your God," i.e., "And you shall teach them diligently to your children": that is, the love for God leads to the love of Torah. The causal connection between the love for God and the love of Israel is self-evident on the basis of R. Zadok's analysis.

Indeed, elsewhere,[5] R. Zadok quotes an interesting responsum of Maharil (R. Jacob Molin, 1360–1427, one of the most important figures in Ashkenazic Jewry), who discusses a question that was asked of his father:

> The Talmud relates: "Simon of Amson would interpret homiletically every *et* [a word that has no innate meaning but precedes every noun that is a direct object] in the

Torah. However, when he came to the verse, *et Hashem Elohekha tira,* 'You shall fear *et* the Lord your God' (Deut. 6:13 and 10:20), he desisted" (*Pesaḥim* 22b) [because one may fear none but God]. Question: why did he not desist when he came upon the verse, "You shall love *et* the Lord your God" (Deut. 6:4)? Answer: there is no limit to love, and one can love every single Jew, as it is written, "You shall love your neighbor as yourself" (Lev. 19:18).

In other words, fear is exclusive: fearing any other source or sovereign diminishes our fear of God. Love, however, is inclusive: loving God leads to love of our neighbors and our fellow human beings.[6] Simon of Amson therefore had no hesitation in interpreting the *et* in that verse too.

R. Zadok's interpretation of "You shall love the Lord your God" thus expands its scope. Without in the least diminishing the leading role in our own lives of our love for God, he interprets this command as embracing as well as love of learning and, most importantly, love of mankind.

CHAPTER 14

R. Samuel David Luzzatto
on "You Shall Love"

Samuel David Luzzatto, popularly known by his acronym, Shadal, was a distinguished early nineteenth-century Italian thinker and exegete whose scholarship was unimpeachable and, in keeping with the Italian tradition, was open to the intellectual and cultural currents of his time. Shadal focuses on our verse, "You shall love the Lord your God," to criticize the rationalist school of Jewish thinkers. In so doing, he sheds additional light on the concept of *ahavat Hashem*.

Shadal begins his critique by challenging the interpretation of *ahavat Hashem* by R. Baḥya, one of the pioneers of Jewish philosophy in the Middle Ages and a man widely revered for his exemplary piety and humanity. For Baḥya, the soul is a simple (i.e., noncomplex) non-material substance that naturally inclines us toward the spiritual. When it is illuminated by the intellect, it strives to serve and obey God (who is utterly spiritual), throwing off the shackles of this world and its illusory pleasures.

Shadal objects to this interpretation not because of any anti-rationalistic bias as such, but because he rejects the ascetic element so prominent in Baḥya's thinking. Indeed, Baḥya's rationalism was accompanied by, and probably resulted in, a degree of asceticism as well as elitism. Because, according to Baḥya, a high level of reasoning is required to "know God" rationally and philosophically, the masses find it difficult both to know

God and, derivatively, to love Him—for, as Baḥya avers, it is the intellect that draws the soul to God and evokes love. Moreover, Baḥya's rationalism posits an inverse relationship between body and soul, matter and spirit; as one ascends, the other descends. Thus, to arrive at a higher spiritual-intellectual plane, one must neglect, even disdain, the body. Shadal considers this ascetic attitude un-Jewish, a stance borrowed from those philosophers (probably referring to the Sufi influence on Baḥya) who look down upon the masses who toil in the daily chores of civilization. The Torah, Shadal maintains, encourages *yishuvo shel olam,* the advancement of civilization. Therefore, neither the love nor the service of God can or ought to be performed in isolation from the world but *within* society where, and where alone, the principles of justice and righteousness can be realized.

Maimonides, too, comes in for his share of criticism by Shadal. In his philosophic work,[1] Maimonides writes that *ahavat Hashem* is unattainable except through a correct perception of reality and the divine wisdom that it reveals. Maimonides, therefore, found it necessary to include the rudiments of the science of his day in his legal code, the *Mishneh Torah.*[2] Shadal considers this attitude, too, as remote from the Torah's view, and he regards these particular chapters as incongruous with the rest of the *Mishneh Torah.* Had Maimonides been a "true philosopher," he writes rather boldly, he would have anticipated that the advance of human civilization and knowledge would supersede the views of Aristotle on natural science and astronomy, making them obsolete. By linking his philosophy in the *Guide* to Aristotelian thought, Maimonides thereby undercuts the validity of his whole system. Shadal declares that though he means no disrespect for Maimonides, he feels obliged to warn the younger generation to think critically and independently, and not rely on contemporary or earlier thinkers merely because they are popular and widely accepted—or because they came earlier in history. The true philosopher, concludes Shadal, relies not on Aristotle or Leibnitz, not on Kant or Hegel or Spinoza, but on Abraham and Moses, on Hillel and R. Akiva.

This does not mean, Shadal adds, that he intends to dissuade his readers or students from secular studies, what we sometimes call *Madda* or general culture, for that "never occurred to my fathers and teachers who were the sages of Italy"; he simply wishes to encourage them to use their critical faculties and to think twice before accepting conventional wisdom. Those who follow the intellectual fads of the day, the "politically correct" attitudes, reveal that they are more interested in honors and in ingratiating themselves with their contemporaries than in searching for the truth.

Shadal reserves his greatest venom for Moses Mendelssohn, the leading philosopher of the Enlightenment, who wrote in the *Be'ur,* his commentary on the Bible, the following apparently innocuous comment on our verse, "You shall love the Lord your God":

> Be happy in your knowledge of His endless perfection, and revel in His faithfulness and oneness, and [your readiness] to do what is good in His eyes—for such is the nature of love.

At first blush there seems nothing exceptionable in this remark. Indeed, it could have been lifted out of the writings of many of the more rationalist Sephardic Rishonim. But Shadal seizes upon this statement as representative of the whole rationalist school and therefore worthy of vigorous refutation. He sees this teaching as an inadmissible amalgam of Greek rationalism and authentic Jewish teaching. Thus, he identifies an inner inconsistency: the first part—"be happy . . . endless perfection"—exemplifies the Greek rationalist approach; the second, "do what is good in His eyes," properly reflects the Jewish spirit.

What is wrong with such a hybrid approach? Shadal maintains that it results in neither philosophy nor Torah. In this particular comment by Mendelssohn, he finds a striking example of this inner contradiction. For if we accept this philosophical (i.e., rationalist) interpretation, we are forced to take a deistic position, according to which God is uninterested in human affairs; for One who is perfect and whose perfection serves no other end save its own is totally self-involved and introverted, a kind of catatonic deity. Moreover, because a deistic framework allows for no relationship or interaction between God and man, everything must be predetermined. In such a totally fatalistic universe, man plays no active role, a view obviously contrary to Torah. Such an outlook leaves no room at all for the genuinely Jewish idea that man should seek to please God by obeying Him. Thus, the first part of Mendelssohn's teaching vitiates the closing clause—that love of God requires that we seek to do that which is pleasing in His eyes.

Having dismissed the various forms of rationalism in interpreting *ahavat Hashem*, Shadal declares that instead of merging Torah and philosophy in an incomplete and unnatural synthesis, we should understand that philosophy and Torah have different goals. Philosophy is the search for truth; Torah is the pursuit of good deeds and moral behavior. If the Torah, for instance, teaches us about the unity of God or the creation of the world, such teachings are not meant to impart either theoretical or scientific truths to us; rather, they should inspire within us the desire to act properly, nobly, obediently. This is why the Torah uses anthropomorphisms (depicting God in corporeal terms) and, especially, anthropopathisms (attributing to Him human emotions): by attributing to God such human affects as anger and love and will and joy, the Torah encourages us to develop a bond with Him. While philosophy appeals to our intellectual faculties, the Torah addresses our innermost feelings; and since humans are composed of both elements, the mental and the emotional, both Torah and philosophy are natural to us. Neither one is invalid; each belongs in its proper sphere. Each is "true" in its own individual context.

When it comes to loving God, therefore, we must engage the Torah on its own terms. Just as love is ascribed to God so that we can encounter and bond with Him in terms we can understand, so does the commandment to love God encourage us to respond to God lovingly by obeying His commandments. For love for God, says Shadal, is not a specific positive commandment, but a collective or general mitzvah very much like the mitzvah of "you shall love the stranger" (Deut. 10:19) or "you shall love your neighbor as yourself" (Lev. 19:18). Such a directive must be understood behaviorally: we are commanded to act *lovingly,* not to love emotionally, for the emotions are in any event not subject to commandment.

Shadal's position is not immune to criticism. Although this is not the place to analyze his views on the relation of Torah and philosophy, the issue is sufficiently related to an understanding of "You shall love the Lord your God" to warrant the comment that his dichotomy between Torah and philosophy is far too neat. In fact, the borderline between them is rather messy and often quite indistinct and cannot be dismissed so airily. Furthermore, his interpretation of *ahavat Hashem* lacks theological force: declaring love a useful fiction hardly inspires religious fervor or the performance of the mitzvot. And on a technical halakhic level, he fails to explain the difference between the specific actional mitzvot and the more generalized commandments, as well as inform us why these latter mitzvot should be reckoned among the 613.

Finally, his behavioral conception of *ahavat Hashem* leaves one uneasy. By contrast, Maimonides, in offering a more affective exegesis of the verse, not only presents us with a more emotionally satisfying explanation of one of the most significant verses in all of Torah, but also one that accords with the literal sense of the passage.[3] Although we find antecedents to Shadal's interpretation of *ahavat Hashem* in Nahmanides' (Ramban) commentary to our verse, that is not enough to exempt Shadal's views from criticism. That *ahavat Hashem* must have pragmatic application goes without saying, but divorcing its expression from genuine religious emotions and profound spiritual sensibilities does an injustice to the *peshuto shel mikra,* the plain sense of the scriptural passage, as well as to generations of saintly Jews who remain enduring models of Jewish piety and ethical conduct.

Yet Shadal has much to teach us in cautioning us against making too easy a synthesis of Torah and whatever is the regnant philosophy of the times. We should especially heed his teaching that Torah endures, whereas secular philosophical thought and scientific theories prove ephemeral. Such warnings can guide us to the proper *kavvanah* as we recite this key verse in the Shema.

CHAPTER 15

Does God Need Our Love?

Now that we have concluded our discussion of the commandment, "You shall love the Lord your God," we turn to a question that often lurks in the darker recesses of our consciousness, too shy to expose itself to the glare of analysis. Yet if we are honest, we must address that question: if indeed God commands us to love Him, does that not in some way betray a *need* in Him to be loved? And does that not imply some lack, some vulnerability or imperfection, in God? And does that not, in turn, run counter to the teaching of the Jewish tradition that God is perfect, absolute, totally autonomous, and in need of nothing or no one?

To respond to this question we must first explore, however briefly, how the Jewish tradition treated the tendency of Scripture to refer to God in human terms.

From ancient days until well into the medieval period, many Jews tended to take the words of the Torah literally. This literalism or "fundamentalism" led many pious Jews to violate some of the most fundamental precepts and concepts in Judaism, such as the incorporeality of God. In the early tannaitic period, reacting against this widespread tendency, the great proselyte, Onkelos, in his classical translation of the Torah into Aramaic, eliminated each and every anthropomorphism and anthropopathism (attributing to God human form or human emotions) by reinterpreting them. In the medieval period, Maimonides fulminated against such base literalism and dedicated a good part of the first third of his immortal *Guide for the Per-*

plexed to reinterpreting such terms. Maimonides argued that such terms were used in the Torah because *dibbrah Torah bi'leshon benei adam,* the Torah speaks in the language of men, i.e., the Torah teaches great religious and philosophical ideas but expresses them metaphorically, in human language, so that we can understand them. However, such figurative language must not be taken literally. Both Onkelos and Maimonides endeavored to purify the faith of Jews from crass and unsophisticated literalisms that tended, in some way or other, to lead them to attribute corporeality, imperfection, or limitation to God. They clearly understood that any assumption that God possesses bodily form, or experiences human needs or wants, is pagan and must be ruthlessly banished. Therefore, in talking about the divine commandment to love God, we must understand that the question we ask is not simple, certainly not simplistic, and that there are indeed grounds in the Jewish tradition to reject the existence of divine "needs"—and yet we must also acknowledge our very human need to speak of God's "needs" in some fashion.

While a confirmed rationalist like Maimonides would find heretical and sacrilegious any talk of such mutual dependence, whether emotional or other, in the divine-human encounter, this would not be the case for those less committed to a rigorous rationalism. This is especially so if we bear in mind that no anthropomorphisms or anthropopathisms are ever meant to be taken at face value. Yet even so, such figures of speech do suggest a real dimension that lies somewhere between the crassly literal and the abstractly metaphoric or symbolic, a dimension that cannot therefore be reduced into a *mere* figure of speech.

To understand this, consider *sympathy* before speaking of love. Love indeed implies a need, a dependency. Sympathy—to feel with or for someone—implies an ability or willingness to understand another's predicament. It is, in this sense, more intellectual and less emotional, such that we are not forced to infer a need in the one who experiences sympathy. Indeed, the prerequisite for love is sympathy; only from such a vantage can one speak of love. And ample precedent exists for the idea that God has sympathy for us,[1] and we for God, troublesome as such notions may at first appear.

The earliest texts already indicate divine sympathy for suffering humanity. The "emotional" aspect of the relationship between God and man is evident in the very beginning of the Torah where, as a result of the divine grant of freedom of the will to the first humans and their failure to use it properly, God experiences something akin to anxiety: "And the Lord repented that He had made man upon the earth, and it grieved Him at His heart" (Gen. 6:6).[2] Now this verse, in all its literalness can be regarded as but an anthropopathism that must be treated as all others. The obvious intent of Scripture is to paint a graphic picture of the tragic consequence of the gap between the "ought" and the "is," between the high, absolute demands of the Creator and the moral frailty of human beings. Divine "grief" in His "heart" is a dramatic way of indicating God's rejection of human conduct.

The Sages of the Mishnah are quite straightforward in acknowledging such divine sympathy for man. On the verse, "In all their affliction He was afflicted" (Isa. 63:9), R. Meir is quoted as saying, "When a man suffers, what does the Shekhinah say? 'My head hurts, My arm hurts.' If God suffers at the blood of the wicked that is shed, how much more so at the blood of the righteous?!" (Mishnah *Sanhedrin* 6:5).

In a truly remarkable text, the Talmud (*Hullin* 60b and *Shevuot* 9a) offers a comment on the words "unto the Lord" in the verse concerning the sin offering on the occasion of Rosh Hodesh, the New Moon: "And one he-goat for a sin offering unto the Lord" (Num. 28:15). The Talmud refers to the well-known aggada that at the beginning of creation the moon and the sun were equally large, but when the moon complained that two sovereigns could not wear one crown and, presumably, argued for its own supremacy over the sun, God ordered the moon to diminish in size and luminescence. That is why, explains the Talmud, the Torah refers to a sin offering "unto the Lord": "Said the Holy One, let this he-goat be an atonement because *I* diminished the moon." At first glance, the plain sense of the text is that God felt that He required atonement because of His draconian decision to diminish the moon; alternatively, even though the moon deserved the punishment, God was sufficiently sympathetic to the moon's plight to feel that He needed atonement.

Rashi relieves the heavily anthropopathic quality of this rabbinic story by commenting that the sin-offering was meant "to appease the moon." Anthropomorphizing the moon is far less troublesome theologically than speaking of God in human terms. Tosafot cites the opinion of the author of *Arukh*, that though it was Israel that needed atonement (for its normal range of misdeeds), it was up to God to set the time for such atonement, and He set it on the New Moon as a way of compensating the moon for its harsh punishment; a similar explanation is given by R. Isaac Alfasi, the Rif.[3] Indeed, so disturbing is this passage that on the margin of the *Shevuot* text we read an unattributed printed comment, "This is one of the secrets of the Kabbalah, and Heaven forbid that it be taken at face value." Nevertheless, if we grant that the incident to which this interpretation of the Numbers verse applies is itself metaphoric—surely a three-way conversation between God, sun, and moon is not meant to be taken literally!—then the notion of God's atonement is similarly not meant literally. Therefore, there is no need to explain away apologetically the otherwise shocking attribution of "sin" to God. Instead, we can understand the intent of the Talmud, namely, to explain that the canons of justice sometimes compel us to do things that are unpalatable, which therefore produce in us a sense of regret at the inevitable negative consequence of administering retaliatory punishment. From this aggadic parable we learn that even God, as it were, wrestles with profound ambivalence in administering justice. His response to this ambivalence—asking that a sin-offering be brought for Him—expresses *divine sympathy for our own ambivalence in facing the unjust execution of justice.* Such divine sympathy implies a fellow feeling, even emotional vulnerability, as it were, on the part of God. We are drawn, therefore, to reciprocate with our own sympathy for our Maker. And it is this morally and spiritually uplifting result that makes acceptable the otherwise problematic notion of divine distress.

The Midrash provides an interesting illustration of this kind of thinking among the Sages.[4] On the verse, "I that speak in *tzedakah,* mighty to save" (Isa. 63:1), an opinion is cited that the *tzedakah*—justice, righteousness, but usually and colloquially charity or any act of special kindness—here referred to is performed *by Israel for God!* Thus the Midrash states: "Which *tzedakah* does the verse intend?—The *tzedakah* you performed for Me when you accepted the Torah, for had you not done so, where would My kingdom be?" A truly startling thought: by accepting the Torah, Israel performed a charitable act toward the Creator! Here, human sympathy for the Creator is projected onto the revelation at Sinai, the covenant itself—the very heart of the Jewish religious historical experience.

The Kabbalists too (especially R. Isaac Luria, "the Ari"), no doubt motivated by the conviction that prayer too often is self-serving and egotistical, teach that prayer intended to fulfill our own needs represents a roundabout expression of *human sympathy for God.* Prayer, after all, should be theocentric, not anthropocentric: just as God suffers for us as He identifies with our pain, so we identify sympathetically with *His pain* and pray for His relief (thus avoiding the embarrassment of appearing to pray for our own petty needs).

Even in contemporary literature, this concept has at times appeared in interesting form. Shmuel Yosef Agnon, Israel's late Nobel laureate, composed a moving *reshut* or introductory petition to the Kaddish, recited by the mourner (as well as several times during formal public worship). The Kaddish begins with the famous words, *Yitgadal ve'yitkadash shemeih rabbah,* "May His great Name be magnified and sanctified." Because it makes no mention of death, the connection between this prayer and mourning has always been puzzling. Agnon's *reshut* provides an explanation. It speaks of the difference between a mortal king and the divine King of all the world. A mortal king, when he goes into battle, is concerned with the overall direction of the war, whether he is winning or losing. He is indifferent to the lives of individual soldiers; they are, basically, mere cannon fodder. The divine King, however, cherishes the life of each and every one of His "soldiers" and considers the death of even a single one a defeat that diminishes His greatness and desecrates His holy Name. Thus, when a human being dies, God has lost a soldier in His divine hosts, and God's Name thereby suffers diminution and desecration. We therefore console God, as it were, by praying for the restoration of His greatness—"May His *great Name be magnified"*—and the sanctification of His Name—"and *sanctified."* For Agnon, the Kaddish is our way of consoling the divine Mourner and expressing our sympathy for Him.[5]

Sympathy, even pity, for God not only finds literary expression but crops up in "real life" as well. The venerable late Mizrahi leader, Shlomo Zalman Shragai, relates in his autobiography[6] an event that touchingly illustrates this capacity for showing sympathy, even pity, for the Creator. Shortly after the Holocaust, Shragai left Warsaw by train and was asked by a friend to look after his elderly father, who was taking the same overnight train to Paris. The elderly gentleman was white, pale, nervous, and deeply melancholy. He refused to answer any of Shragai's questions, keeping silently to himself. After awhile, the old man asked him for help in opening his valise. Inside, Shragai noticed a shofar, some personal articles, and his *tallit* and *tefillin*. Much later, after longer periods of silence, the old man began talking to Shragai. He revealed that he was a Hasid of the Rebbe of Belz from Galicia and had himself suffered horrendously under Hitler. In the middle of the conversation, he stopped and resumed his silence. At dawn, after a fitful sleep, Shragai put on his *tallit* and *tefillin*, but the old man did not. The silence continued for several hours into the afternoon, until the old man suddenly began speaking again. "After all that happened to me and after all that my eyes saw, I refuse to pray to Him. Now I'll get Him angry!" After that—several more hours of silence. Just before nightfall, he turned to Shragai and asked him again to assist him with his baggage. Now he took out his *tallit* and *tefillin* and put them on. After finishing his prayers, he said to Shragai, "By right I shouldn't pray to Him. But doesn't He too need and deserve pity *(rachmones)*? What does He now have left in His world? Who is left to Him? And if He had mercy on me and kept me alive, then He merits that I should take pity on Him, and that is why I finally decided to *davven*." With that, the old man broke out in deep sobbing, crying out in Yiddish, "*Oy, a rachmones oyfn Ribbono shel Olam!*" (Oh, a pity on the Master of the World!) Shragai wept with him, and then they parted from each other.

Other piquant expressions of our sympathy for divine "suffering" can be found in our reaction to God's loneliness, as it were. Much has been written about the reluctance of the ancient pagan world to profess belief in an invisible God; a Deity without a body was too insubstantial for the pagan mind. Perhaps also disturbing to the ancients—and maybe even moderns as well—was the idea of a Deity who existed in utter and absolute aloneness, a solitude that, though exalted and magnificent, was also depressing, bewildering, and unthinkable. Thus just as primitive man, fleshy and physical, found it hard to conceive of a God without body or form, so too such men, dreading loneliness and constitutionally attuned to companionship, resisted the idea of a God resplendent in isolation and seclusion. They wondered: "What does God do all day?" "In whom does He confide?" "With whom does He share His joys and His unhappiness?" They preferred the notion of deities abounding, involved with each other and therefore, like man, fundamentally social beings.

Even after monotheism triumphed over polytheism, there remained a spiritually indigestible aspect of divine oneness: God's utter aloneness.[7] And this lingering leeriness of loneliness must somehow find its expression. This expression, paradoxically, is a solution or at least a palliative for human loneliness. For when we discover the painful reality of our own isolation in the world, we are comforted by our Creator, whose aloneness is of an infinitely higher order.

In the following lines uttered by a deeply religious man on his deathbed in Los Angeles, we find expressed the profound pathos of human loneliness:

> I am dying alone, as nobody can accompany me where I am going. I am "on my own" as never before in my life. But just in this alone-ness which I am facing now, I am closer to God's identity and His alone-ness than ever before. In this true alone-ness I experience and recognize my very own divinity from within in the image of God.[8]

Divine solitude evokes from us our own sense of loneliness in the universe, and not only when we face death. As we meet God, loneliness encounters loneliness; and as each of us offers his loneliness as a gift to the other, we experience relief, as it were, from cosmic loneliness. It is not, of course, that God truly experiences loneliness as we do; we are, certainly, beyond such crude anthropopathisms. Rather, in our religious imagination we project our own loneliness upon God, conceiving of Him too as suffering from this vast and incredible loneliness, and thus allowing man and God to sympathize with each other. As the Sages of Israel put it, in the *tefillin* of Israel it is written, "Hear O Israel, the Lord is our God, the Lord is One"; and in the *tefillin* of God, as it were, are inscribed the words, "Who is like unto Your people Israel, one nation upon the earth?" The communion of the lonely is an antidote to loneliness.[9]

Indeed, the Torah assumes a mutual "dependency" between God and man and their "need" for each other. Thus, the proclamation of divine unity (Deut. 6:4) is followed by the commandment to love Him: "and You shall love the Lord your God with all your heart and all your soul and all your might" (Deut. 6:5). Although divine injunctions to do or obey do not imply God's "need" for us, God does "need" us to love Him.

"The Lord is one" implies that God is, as it were, a lonely God. This loneliness and sadness are reflected in the divine image, humans, of whom He said, "It is not good that man should be alone" (Gen. 2:18). Both God and human beings deserve *rachmones*, pity—we, for our failure and pain and suffering, and God, for being abandoned by this creature created in God's very own image and endowed with the gift of free will that we misuse and abuse. And so each waits and longs for the other. The way to bridge the brooding cosmic loneliness, to find our way to each other, is through—love.

It is this sense of mutual sympathy that gives rise to love. God reaches out for us with love—as affirmed in the blessing immediately preceding the Shema: "Blessed are You, O Lord, who chooses His people Israel *in love"*—and we, recognizing that "the Lord is One," that the Creator is lonely, yearning for our companionship, respond with love immediately after proclaiming God's utter oneness: "You shall *love* the Lord your God with all your heart . . ."

Those thinkers whose interpretations of the Love of God we discussed in chapters 10 to 14 all worked on the premise that God is transcendent and perfect: we need God, but God does not need anyone or anything. He is utterly self-sufficient. But here we are speaking of God in a different way. Conceived of in poetic and psychologically human terms, the divine-human relationship takes on a different dimension, best understood through distinction between two types of love usually referred to in theological writings by their Greek names, *eros* and *agape*.[10] *Agape* is the love that a protective parent feels for his or her child. It is a selfless love: the parent asks nothing in return, not even to be loved by the child. *Eros,* in contrast, is romantic love, such as that felt by husband and wife for each other. Such love is expected to be not only reciprocal, but also mutually pleasurable. The love we feel for and from God is *agape,* not *eros.*

Yet in the Torah and throughout Jewish liturgy, the metaphors describing the love relationship between God and Israel do not reflect such hard and fast distinctions. God is depicted as Father and as King—but also as the Lover of Israel. Solomon's Song of Songs, considered by R. Akiva as holier than all other songs in the Bible, is heretical if we reject *eros* as a model for the love between God and human beings. Isaiah refers to Israel as God's beloved; Hosea freely uses marriage as a metaphor for the God-Israel relationship; and throughout the prophetic writings we find similar analogies. Yet no talmudic eyebrows are raised at these apparently bold anthropopathisms.

Michael Wyschogrod has argued[11] that this bifurcation of love into two distinct categories must be rejected or, at least, seriously questioned from a Jewish perspective. He argues that the Jewish vision of love for God must be understood as both *agape* and *eros*. Although such an approach leaves God, as it were, vulnerable to the vagaries of Israel's temperament and conduct, it has the virtue of making God's love for Israel less abstract and more personal, and it accords with the scriptural description of God as jealous when Israel "goes whoring" after "strange gods." Only in the universe of *eros* do such terms, as well as adultery, divorce, and remarriage, make sense.

Yet we must be wary of taking such images and expressions too literally. For though the rigorous condemnation of any and all anthropomorphisms and anthropopathisms in the Bible and Talmud may sometimes lead to an excessively depersonalized Deity, the opposite tendency is even more dangerous: it may well lead us to form an infantile conception of a corporeal god, blurring the differences between the divine Creator and His human creatures.

How can we arrive at a position that satisfies both the theological demands of monotheistic purity and the psychological need for putting a "human face" on religious experience? Rabbi Leon (Aryeh) de Modena Italy (1571–1648), in his *Ari Nohem,* provides a useful analogy in a slightly different context: A sailor on an incoming vessel approaches the pier and throws his line to those who stand on the pier. After they tie the line to the pier, the sailor tugs on the line in order to pull himself and his craft toward the pier so that he can disembark. To the onlooker, the sailor is *pulling the pier toward himself,* whereas in fact *he is pulling himself to the pier.* So, when we speak of God's "needs"—for compassion or companionship or love or relief from distress—we are in reality pulling ourselves to Him, i.e., expressing our own deepest feelings and needs and projecting them upon Him as an act of communion as we cleave to Him.

For a more sophisticated explanation of this point, it would be useful at this time to revisit an important distinction that engaged us earlier, in chapter 7. The first verse of the Shema, according to R. Shneur Zalman and R. Ḥayyim of Volozhin, alludes to the exclusive ontological reality of God. That is, nothing else can be said to truly exist; all that is non-divine is mere illusion. But the verse *Barukh shem kevod* that we recite immediately afterward, in keeping with rabbinic tradition, assures us that the world we inhabit *does* exist, and so we must act accordingly. Borrowing a distinction first formulated by the sixteenth-century Safed Kabbalist R. Moshe Cordovero, R. Shneur Zalman and R. Ḥayyim of Volozhin explain that this apparent contradiction is resolved by assigning the Shema verse to *mi-tziddo,* from God's point of view, and the rabbinic verse to *mi-tziddenu,* from our point of view. Thus, in the most fundamental sense, reality can be ascribed only to God; however, it is *His will* that we mortals, bound inextricably in this web of illusion, close our eyes to the cosmos' ultimate unreality and act *as if* it were all real. So it is that we first affirm the abstract proposition that nothing but God exists, that our world is devoid of all ontological validity. Then we return to our "everyday" world of sensate experience and human needs and declare that we are both real and worthy to serve God. We accept this world as real because of our human need to do so *and* because God has willed that we act this way, as if "God is in Heaven and we are on earth." In the course of living our lives *mi-tziddenu,* we thus confront and engage God as if we were "real" beings, participating in "true" existence.

In similar fashion, we acknowledge that from the point of view of ultimate reality—understood fully only by God and only asserted philosophically but never fully comprehended existentially by human beings—we can never attribute such imperfections as need, injury, vulnerability, and loneliness to God; God is beyond all emotion, including love. Nevertheless, in our daily lives as thinking, feeling, and active beings, we relate to God *psychologically* as a sentient, feeling, reacting Being.

Approaching God this way respects Onkelos's and Maimonides' strictures against anthropopathisms (and certainly anthropomorphisms), yet allows us to go beyond the realm of metaphor, to nurture our relationship to God in an existentially and psychologically more meaningful way than merely poetic or metaphoric analogy. The Cordoveran paradigm resolves the conflict between the philosophers and those ordinary religious folk (and some extraordinary ones as well!) for whom prayer is more than poetry, and love more than metaphor. It allows us to keep our hearts without losing our heads. And it tells us that, yes, God needs our love as surely as we need His. If this understanding emerges as only "from our point of view," so be it, for it is quite presumptuous—and impossible—to view anything "from God's point of view."

PART III

Verses 3–6

CHAPTER 16

"With All Your Heart and All Your Soul and All Your Might"

"With All Your Heart"

In the psychology of both Bible and Talmud, the heart is regarded as a complex organ, the seat both of the intellect and of emotion and attitude (as in colloquial usage today). The expressions, a "good heart" and a "bad heart," refer not to cardiological conditions, but to our moral-cognitive disposition. In rabbinic writing, the heart is the locus of two dramatically conflicting tendencies or impulses, one urging us toward good actions, the other toward evil. Each of these urges is called a *yetzer,* from the root *y-tz-r,* to create, probably because a human being, as a creation (*YeTZuR*) of God (the *YoTZeR*), possesses the right and duty to choose between these two warring urges, the Good Urge *(yetzer ha-tov)* and the Evil Urge *(yetzer ha-ra).* Indeed, the whole moral enterprise of human life can be described as an ongoing contest between these urges— the good and the evil, the constructive and the destructive, the noble and the malevolent.

In one of the most well-known commentaries of the Rabbis, the Sifre[1] applies this duality to the verse commanding us to love God "with all your heart," interpreting the double *bet* of the Hebrew word for heart, *levavkha,* as indicating that we are to love God not only with our Good Urge, our moral instincts, but also with our *yetzer ha-ra,* our Evil Urge.[2]

What does it mean to love God with our *yetzer ha-ra*? To a contemporary person, this idea has immediate resonance. It anticipates Freud's well-known theory of sublimation, that is, the redirection of the id's libidinal forces from their erotic goals to more culturally and socially useful ones, such as the creation of art, technology, and literature. Although it is doubtful that Freud ever heard of the Sifre, his theory echoes in modern form an idea at least 2,000 years old, modified with his own particular stamp on it. For Jewish tradition, this interpretation of "with all your heart" is not merely a homiletic *bon mot* noteworthy for its charm. Rather, it represents a major tendency within the Jewish tradition's psychology of the soul.

Commenting on God's words uttered after the creation of man, "and God saw everything that He had made, and behold it was very good" (Gen. 1:31), the Midrash (Genesis Rabbah, 9:9) explains:

> "And behold it was . . . *good*" refers to the Good Urge; "and behold it was *very* good" refers to the Evil Urge. But can the Evil Urge be considered "very good"? Astonishing! But [what this means is that] if not for the Evil Urge a man would not build a house or marry a woman or sire children or engage in business.

Thus our midrash teaches that our destructive powers, in their primal origin, not only have the capacity to be redirected for constructive purposes, but indeed are *far more potent* than the positive ethical and moral dispositions innate within human nature. The good is *good,* but the evil—used for the good—is even better: in fact, it is *very good.* This approach was later to be developed more fully in Hasidism.[3] But this rabbinic theory of sublimation represents only one traditional approach to the problem of internal evil. The more normative "classical" approach takes an altogether different tack: we act to fight evil and attempt to destroy it.

In an attempt to integrate these two traditional views of evil, R. Shneur Zalman[4] proposes that there are two types of righteous persons, the *tzaddik gamur* ("the completely righteous person") and the *benoni* ("the intermediate person"). The former has attained such a high moral-spiritual plane that he has successfully extirpated every remnant of evil from within himself, converting it to the good. In contrast, the latter, though utterly sinless, nonetheless harbors the *desire* to sin, so that he must endlessly struggle with it.

According to R. Shneur Zalman's typology, the *tzaddik gamur* and the *benoni* differ as well in the way they approach evil within themselves. The *benoni* strives to conquer his negative impulses, to cast them away with both hands, in an effort R. Shneur Zalman calls *itkafia,* the suppression of the *yetzer ha-ra.* For the *benoni,* the battle is never over. With dogged persistence, the *yetzer ha-ra* keeps on returning to its task. (One recalls the Talmud's comment that the *yetzer ha-ra* is like a fly and R. Israel Salanter's interpretation—that just as a fly keeps on returning, no matter how often you chase it away, so too does the *yetzer ha-ra.*) R. Shneur Zalman counsels the *benoni* not to be discouraged by the rigors of this endless battle, for this effort in itself is pleasing to the Creator.

The *tzaddik gamur,* however, approaches the internal evil of man differently. He follows the path not of *itkafia* but of *it'hapkha,* of conversion or sublimation: rather than suppress or banish the powers of the *yetzer,* he exploits them for the good. R. Shneur Zalman calls it "the conversion from bitter to sweet and from dark to light." The *yetzer ha-ra* is thereby transformed into a positive and constructive force, which, of course, is certainly pleasing to the Holy One.[5]

R. Shneur Zalman adds a note of caution to his elaboration of these two approaches to evil. The spiritual standards he establishes to qualify as a *benoni*—a person of only middling righteousness—are so high, so demanding, that it is the rare individual in a generation who can attain them; those expected of a *tzaddik gamur* are clearly out of the reach of most mortals. Thus, the *it'hapkha* method is appropriate only for the rare saint; the rest of us who hope some day to attain even spiritual mediocrity should be happy simply to attempt to practice *itkafia*. For when *it'hapkha* is attempted by someone unqualified, it can lead to dangerous results, namely, falling even deeper into the clutches of sin instead of overpowering it. This fear is not unrealistic. Indeed, such antinomian, even diabolical reversals of character are well documented in history.

All these interpretations, beginning with that of the Sifre, assume an undifferentiated striving or potency at the root of the human psyche—what Freud called the libido—that activates the constructive impulse *(yetzer ha-tov)*, but more often the destructive impulse *(yetzer ha-ra)*. Because both impulses originate in a common source, it is possible, albeit with great effort, to convert one form of striving into the other. This conception assumes that the Evil Urge derives not from any objective, external evil but from an internal, intrinsic need or desire that has become corrupted because in its expression it violates the divine norm. For our grasping nature, our lust and insatiable appetites, are not innately bad; they can be directed or redirected to constructive ends. But if these drives are expressed untrammeled and unguided by our moral sense or our submission to divinely revealed norms, they are evil—in a relative, not in an absolute or ontological sense.

This monistic understanding of the *yetzer*, linked to an interpretation of our biblical verse, "with all your heart," is not, however, universally accepted. Maimonides offers an alternative interpretation of this phrase that echoes the Mishnah's teaching that one must offer a blessing for bad news as well as for good news (*Berakhot* 9:1). The Mishnah's proof-text is our passage, interpreted to mean that the phrase "with all your heart" refers both to the Good and the Evil Urge, demonstrating that they are separate from and not convertible to each other. Maimonides[6] explains that we must therefore implant in our hearts love for and faith in God even at the very time we are filled with rebellion, anger, and fury (against God), for as the Sages teach in reference to the verse, "In all your ways know Him" (Prov. 3:6), we must know God "even with a sin."[7] This dualistic view of the *yetzer* yields a psychologically cogent insight that acknowledges the complexity and vagaries of the human soul: that one must love God and believe in Him even while sinning, for transgression does not necessarily arise from the denial of God or any other heretical ideological reasons, but rather from the divided self.

The Maharal of Prague offers another thoroughly dualistic interpretation of "with all your heart" without referring to the Sifre at all. For the Maharal, to love God requires that we devote ourselves totally to the Holy One with every part of our being. The Sages always maintained that there exists within every human being an element of pure evil, a lust for evil for its own sake and not merely to slake one's appetites:

> Man possesses a longing for that which is evil because it is evil, not merely because of some pleasure he feels he needs. It is only because of his longing for that which is evil.[8]

According to the Maharal, this pursuit of evil, motivated by our fascination with it or by some innate corruption of the human soul, is what the Talmud calls *yetzer ha-ra*. Thus, to love God "with all your heart" means that we direct our entire psychological and spiritual constitution in the service of that love. To do so requires that we first remove all evil and lust for evil from within ourselves.

The Maharal's pessimistic view of the human propensity for evil—objective, intrinsic evil that is part of human nature, not merely the subjective, relative, convertible kind—should resonate with us in this post-Holocaust era. For the Holocaust unmasked the evil face of Western civilization. It laid bare the futility of science, art, and education, the vanity of believing that two thousand years of preaching love and turning the other cheek could ensure at least a minimally safe and secure life. Even more, it stripped bare our pitiful soul, exposing all its ugliness and brutality along with the redeeming features with which its Creator endowed it. I am reminded of the late Isaac Bashevis Singer's short story, "The Last of the Demons," in which the demon announces: "I am the last of the demons. Who needs demons any more now that man does our work?"[9]

What the Holocaust taught us, reinforcing and amplifying the ugly lessons already drilled into us by human history, is that evil is also intrinsic and objective. In confronting this evil, therefore, we have no recourse but to meet it head on and attempt to overcome it, uproot it, banish it utterly and totally; if the contest must go on endlessly, so be it. For this kind of evil cannot simply be elevated or sanctified or converted; it is so "bitter" and "dark" that it can never be transmuted into "sweet" and "light."

For R. Shneur Zalman and many other hasidic masters, the Sifre's comment—that the commandment to love God "with all your heart" means serving the Lord with both urges—must be understood ideally as the sublimation of an evil that is fundamentally chimerical and insubstantial, that is, in fact, nothing but a vehicle for the good. Yet even this monistic, redemptive view acknowledges that for the overwhelming majority of mankind, the very best of whom—with rare exceptions—qualify only for the status of *benoni*, the "intermediately righteous person," such sublimation is unattainable. Our efforts must therefore be directed to the suppression of the evil within us.

Maharal is less charitable and more pessimistic. He does not even mention the interpretation of the Sifre, for not even theoretically will he grant that *yetzer ha-ra* and *yetzer ha-tov* originate from a common source, that the good and evil within us are just two sides of the same coin. In his dualistic view, evil is real, hard, ugly, irreducible, non-negotiable, and unconvertible. To love God with all our heart requires that we confront that inner evil, that lust for evil for its own sake, realistically and courageously, that we recognize it for what it is, giving it no quarter in our incessant efforts to vanquish it.

"With All Your Soul"

R. Akiva taught that the words "with all your soul" imply accepting martyrdom for the sake of the love of God: one must love God "even though He takes your soul."

Two parallel texts dramatize the fascinating and tragic context of this teaching; the differences between the two are instructive. The first passage is found in the Babylonian Talmud:

> The Rabbis taught: Once the evil kingdom [i.e., the Romans] decreed that the Jews may not engage in the study of Torah. Pappus b. Yehuda came and found R. Akiva publicly assembling large groups [of Jews] and engaging in [the study of] Torah. He said to him, "Akiva, are you not afraid of the authorities?" . . . When [the Romans] took R. Akiva to execute him, it was the time for the reading of the Shema. They were tearing his flesh with iron combs, and he

was accepting upon himself the yoke of the Kingdom of Heaven [i.e., reciting the Shema]. His disciples said to him: "O Rabbi, so much?" [i.e., must one go so far in suffering for the sake of Torah?]. Said he to them: "All my life I was troubled by the verse, "With all your soul," which [I interpret as] 'even if He takes your soul,' wondering: when will I have the opportunity to fulfill it? Now that I have that opportunity, shall I not fulfill it?" He [recited the Shema and] prolonged [his articulation of the word *eḥad* [One] until he expired [while saying the word] *eḥad*. Whereupon a heavenly voice proclaimed, "Happy are you, R. Akiva, for your soul has departed with [the declaration of] *eḥad*. (*Berakhot* 61b)

The second and parallel account comes from the Jerusalem Talmud:

R. Akiva was brought to trial before the Tyrant Rufus *[tyrannus Rufus]*. The time for the recitation of the Shema arrived, and [R. Akiva] read the Shema and smiled. Tyrant Rufus said to him: "Old man, either you are a magician [and therefore do not feel the torture] or you ignore suffering" [perhaps implying that he was a masochist]. Said [R. Akiva] to him: "May your breath leave you! I am neither a magician nor one who is indifferent to pain. It is, rather, that all my life I have recited [the Shema] and was troubled by one verse, wondering when I would have the opportunity [to fulfill] the three [elements in it]—'You shall love the Lord your God with all your heart and all your soul and all your possessions.'[10] I have loved Him with all my heart and I have loved Him with all my possessions, but I was not [yet] tested as to my soul. Now that I have reached [this stage where I am to surrender] 'all your soul,' and the time for the Reading of the Shema has arrived, I shall not be distracted from loving Him! That is why I recite—and smile." He barely finished speaking [these words] when his soul soared upwards. (J. *Berakhot* 9:5)

In both the Babylonian and the more elaborate Jerusalem versions of this event, R. Akiva interprets "with all your soul" as implying martyrdom, giving up of one's soul or life for the love for God. But a number of differences between them—two literary, and one more substantive—deserve mention.

In the account in the Babylonian Talmud, R. Akiva relates his *derashah* (interpretation) to his disciples. In contrast, in the Palestinian version, he directs his comments to the enemy himself, indicating a readiness openly to challenge and taunt his tormentor. Similarly, the Babylonian Talmud makes no mention of R. Akiva smiling or laughing, whereas in the Jerusalem Talmud the smile is significant. The smile seems to be of a double nature—part pleasure at performing a mitzvah (that of *kiddush Hashem*, martyrdom, "even if He takes your soul"), part smirk and contempt for the tyrant.

A further and more important difference: The Babylonian version highlights the time for reading the Shema as the essential element of the tale. It focuses on the biblical proof-text as the source for requiring such an act of martyrdom. Note the wording of the text: "When [the Romans] took R. Akiva to execute him, it was the time for the Reading of the Shema." The Rabbis here reinforce the idea that R. Akiva's invocation of the phrase "with all your soul" and his death upon reciting *ehad* teach us not only that his martyrdom coincided with the Reading of the Shema, but that *martyrdom itself is an aspect* of reading the Shema, as R. Akiva taught all his life and, ultimately, with his death.

In the Jerusalem Talmud's version, the Reading of the Shema, though important, is not quite central to the dramatic tension of the story. When the time for reading the Shema arrives fortuitously as R. Akiva is being interrogated and tortured by

Rufus, R. Akiva uses this very moment to flaunt a sardonic smile and heroically defy the tyrant. But R. Akiva's death was primarily a fulfillment not of the mitzvah of reading the Shema, but that of accepting martyrdom ("even if He takes your soul"). This mitzvah applies to all times and places and is independent of any recitation. As R. Akiva defiantly asserts: "Now that I have reached [this stage where I am to surrender] 'all your soul,' and the time for the Reading of the Shema has arrived, I shall not be distracted from loving Him! That is why I recite—and smile," as if to emphasize his satisfaction that he can, *at one and the same time*, simultaneously fulfill two important but separate mitzvot: martyrdom *and* reading the Shema, especially the verse "with all your soul."

Perhaps the discrepancies between these two versions of R. Akiva's death highlight an implicit difference of halakhic approach between the two Talmuds (although this is offered only as a suggestion on the basis of a rather subtle literary analysis of the two versions). In concentrating primarily on R. Akiva's martyrdom as a fulfillment of his *derashah* on the "with all your soul" verse of the Shema, the Babylonian Talmud implies that the mitzvah of *kiddush Hashem* is achieved at the moment one is *ready* to die for God's sake, even if one does not actually suffer martyrdom; it is the psychological readiness to surrender one's life that constitutes the mitzvah. R. Akiva, who has always been prepared to die for the love of God, can now prove his *bona fides:* "Now that I have that opportunity, shall I not fulfill it?" His martyrdom fulfills the mitzvah he has always performed when reading this verse of the Shema, namely, his readiness to suffer death every time he recited the verse. His death retroactively validates his sincere intention to suffer death for his faith. But it was halakhically not necessary that he actually die in order to fulfill the requirements of the mitzvah; it was enough that he sincerely declare his willingness to love God "even if He takes your soul."

The Jerusalem Talmud, however, in stressing R. Akiva's simultaneous performance of the two separate mitzvot, implies that the mitzvah of *kiddush Hashem* is achieved only at the moment one actually *dies* for God's sake. Although psychologically surrendering one's life when reading the Shema *prepares* one for martyrdom, the full performance of the mitzvah takes place only when the martyr actually suffers death. In R. Akiva's case, he was able to perform the two mitzvot simultaneously— reading the Shema and suffering martyrdom—but the two are not integrally related.

Later sources express support for both these views. Thus, the Zohar writes:

> Whoever intends with these words [i.e., "you shall love . . . with all your soul"] to surrender his life for the sanctification of the divine Name, Scripture considers it as if he was martyred every day [that he recited these words with this *kavvanah*]. (Zohar III, 195b)

This passage reinforces the view that we have attributed to the Babylonian Talmud. Other sources espouse this point of view as well. But some sources take the opposite view, siding with the perspective implied in the version of the Jerusalem Talmud.

Whether or not the *intention* to undergo martyrdom adequately fulfills the mitzvah formally, it is clear that such an intention is an integral part of the Reading of the Shema. We then are faced with an interesting question: to what extent must we pursue this mitzvah? Should we seek out opportunities to tempt fate and expose ourselves to danger in order to demonstrate our love of God? Not all authorities agree on the answer to this question.

R. Isaiah Horowitz (end of the sixteenth and beginning of the seventeenth century), in his *Shenei Luḥot ha-Berit*,[11] one of the most significant works in all of Jewish literature, expresses strong opinions on the matter:

> One should not think that because martyrdom is a great mitzvah, therefore I will pursue it diligently, in the same way that one must diligently pursue every (other) mitzvah, and I will try to create a situation [that will result in my martyrdom], such as: when he sees a pagan he will spit at him, or visit other such indignities upon him, so that they will seize him and burn him at the stake. . . .
>
> One who acts in this manner is guilty [of forfeiting] his life. The mitzvah [of martyrdom] applies only to a case where [the violation of one of the three commandments requiring martyrdom] was forced upon him by others; only then shall he sanctify the Name and prefer to be killed rather than violate [one of these commandments].

That is, we must not seek out opportunities to die a martyr's death. Such active solicitation of martyrdom is a disguised form of suicide and must be discouraged. We can only conjecture about the historical circumstances that may have inspired this vigorous condemnation of pro-active martyrdom.

The Netziv (R. Naftali Zevi Yehuda Berlin) concurs: "Heaven forbid that R. Akiva hoped for such a terrible death."[12] The Netziv's nephew, R. Baruch Epstein, apparently unaware of his uncle's comment, takes the opposite view. Citing an incident recorded about R. Akiva in the Talmud,[13] he contends that R. Akiva did indeed anticipate and hope for a martyr's death.[14] The plain sense of the passage in both Talmuds seems to support the view of R. Epstein.

"With All Your Might"

Most English-language prayer books translate *u-ve'khol me'odekha* as "with all your might," a translation undoubtedly derived from the King James translation of the Bible. Although none of the standard Jewish exegetes explains the word that way, it is nevertheless a legitimate translation of the word, for reasons that will become clear presently.

The Talmud interprets *me'odekha*, first, as "your money" *(kol mamonkha)*[15] or "possessions" (so, for instance, Onkelos: *u-ve'khol nikhsakh*). The second translation is more of an interpretation: "no matter what destiny He metes out to you, thank Him" (a play on the words *me'od-middah-modeh*). Both talmudic explanations of the word are cited by Rashi in his Bible commentary.[16] Leaving aside the second interpretation as more homiletic than literal, we are left with two alternative translations: "might" or "money/possessions." There is, however, no need to choose between them. Ramban and Ibn Ezra before him both point to the obvious origin of the word as *me'od,* "very."[17] For Ibn Ezra, the phrase translates into "love Him very very much"; Ramban reconciles this understanding with the rabbinic term *mamon,* "money," related either conceptually or etymologically—Ramban can be read both ways—to *hammon,* "multitude" or "large numbers." "Very-ness" is thus akin to "money" or possessions. Ramban also relates *me'od* to *hayyil,* which means "wealth," both of numbers and of substance, and also implies power or might. The word is often translated as "hosts" (indicating large numbers) while at the same time implying the power that comes with large numbers. So, *hayyil* means "soldier" and, in slightly different contexts, simply "might." All the three alternative meanings—money, might, and multitude—are related to each other, and all derive, directly or indirectly, from the concept of *me'od,* "very."

We are commanded to love God with "all your very-ness"—with all we have that speaks of power and possessions.[18]

Now, if indeed "with all your might" means that we must express our love for God by sacrificing our material means, how far must we go in doing so? What, in other words, are the halakhic guidelines that define and limit this obligation?

R. Baruch Epstein[19] raises the question of whether we are halakhically required, on this basis, to abandon all our possessions and be reduced to utter penury if forced to violate any negative commandment. Is such extreme financial self-sacrifice mandated to avoid any and every transgression, or does it apply only to the cases of the three cardinal sins—murder, idolatry, and certain categories of sexual immorality—concerning which we are instructed *yehareg ve'al yaavor,* it is preferable to submit to martyrdom? If the latter is the case, then "with all your might/money" carries the same demands as "with all your soul," but not more than that. That is, we need to surrender all our worldly goods, as well as to submit to martyrdom, *only* to avoid committing the three cardinal sins.

The most extreme opinion, that of R. Moses Isserles (Rema), author of the famous glosses to the universally accepted Code of Jewish Law, the *Shulḥan Arukh,* requires we abandon all our material possessions for the sake of our faith, or our love for God, and not only in the case of the three most serious sins. Without identifying them by name, he cites certain Rishonim (Talmudists of the medieval era) who hold that in order to avoid transgressing any negative commandment, we must be prepared to surrender all we possess. Rema does not distinguish between the three major negative commandments mentioned and the entire gamut of 365 such negative mitzvot.[20]

R. Epstein questions this decision, basing his opposition on a passage in the Talmud (*Berakhot* 61b) that records the Rabbis' puzzlement about why, after being commanded to risk our lives ("with all your soul") for God, we now have to be commanded to risk our substance as well: surely, if we accept the former obligation, is it not self-evident that we commit ourselves to the latter? The Rabbis respond with a paradoxical but realistic psychological insight: some people would prefer to yield their lives rather than their substance; such people must be made to understand that they have to be ready to sacrifice not only their lives but *also their money*. In this passage, the Talmud establishes the equivalence of the phrases "with all your soul" and "with all your might/money." Therefore, just as the former is operative only with regard to the three major transgressions, so too is the latter. For losing all our worldly goods and being reduced to mendicancy is as devastating as losing our lives. We thus should not sacrifice all our worldly possessions under duress *(o'nes)* except in the case of the three cardinal sins. Such indeed is the decision of R. Abraham Abele Gombiner,[21] who rules that if confronted by robbers who threaten to take all our possessions on Shabbat, leaving us utterly destitute, we are permitted to violate the Sabbath in order to resist, because such financial devastation is tantamount to *pikuaḥ nefesh,* a risk to life itself. With some hesitancy, R. Epstein inclines to this view over that of Rema.[22]

Having touched on the phrase "with all your might" from a halakhic perspective, we will now turn to two homiletical but equally compelling insights, the first by a leading hasidic thinker who was radical in his interpretation of our phrase and whose comments are consistent with the general *Weltanschauung* of the hasidic movement; and the second by his younger contemporary, a leading mitnagdic Talmudist and Torah commentator.

The hasidic master, R. Zadok Hakohen of Lublin,[23] maintains that "with all your might/money" means that we must be so filled with *ahavat Hashem* (love for God) that this love overflows into our very possessions so that they too, inanimate as they are, glow with our love of God. That is why the Sages taught that the donkey of the Tanna R. Pinḥas b. Yair ate no forbidden foods; the sanctity of its master was carried over to the animal. Of course, attaining such a spiritual level is rare indeed, which is why the Torah included "with all your might/money" in the first paragraph of the Shema, formulated in the singular and thus directed to individuals, but not in the second paragraph, written in the plural and addressed to all Jews, those incapable of such spiritual excellence. Only the truly unique individuals arrive at a state whereby all they possess is elevated to the level of holy articles—such as the scroll of the Torah or *tefillin*—for through such things they spread *ahavat Hashem* in the world.

Here we encounter the hasidic concept of *shoresh ha-nefesh*, the "Root of the Soul." According to hasidic teaching, the soul is located in an environment or spiritual neighborhood that determines our situation in mundane life. Thus "all that man possesses—his wife and children, his servant and maid, his animals and home, his gold and his silver, all that he owns—all of this comes from the Root of his Soul."[24] This belief derives from hasidic immanentism, the view that divinity inheres in everything, that (in the words of the Zohar) "there is no place that is free of Him." This is how Hasidism understands the literal and therefore real meaning of the prophet's declaration that "the world is filled with His glory" (Isa. 6:3). Not only does divinity inhere in the human soul and intellect, but—as R. Isaac Luria had said—in every object in the world, no matter how lowly.

Thus, even material objects have a spiritual origin or core; we can speak of them as having a source in the empyrean realms. So, just as friendship in the here-and-now "reveals" the propinquity of the "Roots of the Souls" to each other in the world of the spirit, so too are we related to our most cherished physical possessions in a spiritual manner: the Roots of human Souls are close indeed to the soul-roots of our inert possessions. In this manner, R. Zadok and other hasidic masters speak of a person's *ahavat Hashem* being revealed through his or her material possessions.[25] For if a person is truly devout, if his *ahavat Hashem* is genuine, then somehow, marvelously, this love will shine through the most mundane and inanimate objects in his possession.[26]

Finally, let us look at an interpretation by R. Meir Simha of Dvinsk, Latvia, in his great commentary, the *Meshekh Hokhmah* (to Deut. 6:5). He regards the word *me'od*, "very," as indicating excess: "more" or "extra." Our very-ness, our *me'od*, is that which we, as human beings, possess and which lower species do not. R. Meir Simha identifies that extra "something" as the ability to abide present difficulties for the sake of future benefits—something of which animals are incapable. It is with this talent to defer current gratification that we must love God: "hence . . . even though He punishes us, we must know that it is all for the sake of some future good, whether it be the forgiveness of sins [through suffering] or the purification of our material selves, and the like-matters known to Providence alone."

Thus, we must humanize the very act of loving God as *me'od*: we must love even when that love is as yet unrequited, confident that ultimately it will be acknowledged, accepted, and reciprocated. Religious people thus take a great risk in offering their emotions, their lives, their distinctiveness to a God who sometimes seems not to care; yet that is what makes them all the more human. Our capacity to be vulnerable and to defer gratification demonstrates not only our psychological maturity but also our spiritual growth.

CHAPTER 17

The Torah, the Heart, and Education

Following the initial commandment to love God with all our being, the first paragraph of the Shema now continues:

> And these words which I command you this day shall be upon your heart; and you shall teach them diligently to your children, and you shall talk of them when you sit in your house and when you walk by the way, when you lie down and when you rise up.

"*These words* which I command you this day" is rather ambiguous. What is the antecedent of "these words": The words of the Shema up to this point? All the words of the Shema? The words of the Torah in general?

When they draw upon this passage as a source of halakhic discussion and analysis, the talmudic Sages take "these words" to mean the words of the Shema itself. That is, the Torah here instructs us how to read the Shema. But when the Rabbis expand the scope of "these words" to encompass the entirety of the Torah, they move beyond halakhic technicality into the realm of spiritual, ethical, and psychological instruction—much of which helps orient us when the Shema is recited. We shall analyze the verses for such enlightenment phrase by phrase, although obviously a great many of the commentaries in the sources refer to more than one phrase at a time.

"These Words"

The halakhic interpretation of our passage originates in the Mishnah (*Berakhot* 2:1), which discusses what happens when, in the course of studying Deuteronomy, the reader comes across and recites the passages we call the Shema. The Mishnah teaches that the reader does not fulfill the requirement of "Reading of the Shema" as a religious duty unless he specifically *intended* to fulfill that particular mitzvah. A casual reading of these verses, without *kavvanah,* is inadequate; one must repeat the Shema with the proper thoughts in mind.

The Gemara (*Berakhot* 13a, b), elaborating on this cryptic remark of the Mishnah, goes on to ask how much of the Shema requires *kavvanah:* the entire first paragraph or only up to "these words"? Or does this stricture perhaps imply not that this first part of the Shema alone requires intention, the rest of the first paragraph requiring enunciation ("reading") even without intention, but rather the opposite: that *kavvanah* is mandated for the entire paragraph, but "reading" (aloud) is required only up to the phrase "these words"? The Halakha decides that only the very first verse, "Hear O Israel," requires intention (in the sense of knowing what one is saying).[1]

"Your Heart"

As previously mentioned, "these words" that are to be placed "upon your heart" refer to the whole corpus of divine revelation, that is, to Torah. What, we must then ask, is the relation between the words of the Torah and the human heart? How do the words of Torah—austere and magnificent, ancient and transcendent—connect with our innermost being?

The heart, in the Bible, is the seat of both intellect and emotion, of reason and intention, of the Good Urge and the Evil

Urge. In other words, it is the source of personality and character. The prophet Ezekiel (38:10) points to the heart's capacity for evil intentions as he rails at Gog: ". . . It shall also come to pass that at the same time shall things come into your heart and you shall think an evil thought." Or, even more to the point is this brooding and angry statement by Jeremiah (17:9): "The heart is deceitful above all things, and desperately wicked; who can know it?" This verse occasioned the following comment by the Rabbis: All of the organs of man remain more or less as God created them, except for the heart. "Said Jeremiah, [the heart] changes from hour to hour, and man changes his self and makes himself crooked."[2]

Thus, our verse in the Shema urges that the divine words be placed "upon your heart," so that they decisively influence our actions and behavior for the good and the honorable instead of being "deceitful . . . and desperately wicked."

But at this point we encounter a more acute problem. To take the words of the Shema seriously, especially as commented and elaborated upon by the talmudic and midrashic Sages, confronts us with a formidable dilemma: On the one hand, if we take the injunctions of the Shema as hyperbole, as Scripture's dramatic way of making a point, we cannot really hope to understand what the Torah truly requires of us. But on the other hand, to accept them as they are, in all their stark literalness, is an overpowering experience. How can we, in truth, expect to "love the Lord your God with all your heart and all your soul and all your might?" And if we accept the Rabbis' expansion of these terms, is it at all possible to fulfill this fundamental commandment? Who indeed has the spiritual strength and psychic capacity to sublimate all libidinal impulses and redirect them for so remote a goal as loving God? Are we prepared to give up our lives and our fortunes in order to prove that love? Is such profound commitment possible, especially in an age so critical of "the true believer," so cynical about the extent of human spirituality, so suspicious about all claims that point to the transcendent, beyond the material or the "scientifically" provable?

Before we address this question, let us consider an apparently insignificant literary problem that may guide us toward an answer. Our verse contains a rather awkward preposition in the phrase "*upon* your heart." Most contemporary editions translate this as, "*in* your heart," which is the obvious sense of the text. But the Hebrew is not *bi'levavekha*, "in" your heart, but *al levavekha*, "upon" your heart. The King James version, from which we have quoted above, is closer to the literal reading of the text. Is this expression simply an idiomatic peculiarity, or does it hold some hidden meaning?

The hasidic master R. Zadok Hakohen of Lublin elaborates on this stylistic oddity.[3] The heart, says R. Zadok, is never neutral; it never rests. It is either preoccupied with thoughts of Torah, or it is filled with *hirhurim*, that is, ignoble, unworthy thoughts. While Torah is identical with *emet*, truth—an intellectual category—random thoughts (the *hirhurim*) are a function of the human being's imaginative faculties: wide-ranging and undisciplined, fanciful and poetic, charming and deceitful, full of sacred potential and yet equally capable of the most dangerous self-delusion.

However, these terms are relative. One person's "Torah," his profound and true intellectual apprehension, may be mere "imagination" from the perspective of a superior mind. Yet such understanding of Torah, though limited, should not be deprecated, for it often presents truths that are accepted on faith alone. Regardless of how they are arrived at, they are true nonetheless.

Indeed, herein lies the difference between Moses and all other true prophets. *Prophecy*, which occupies a lower rung than *wisdom*, must employ the imaginative faculty because the prophet can only intuit, suggest, and teach by indirection, by symbol and metaphor. The truths he wishes to impart may be beyond his cognitive grasp; they are usually too abstruse to communicate to others. Hence his extensive use of metaphor and image. Moses, however, because he attained the heights of "wisdom," was able to dispense with "imagination." His vision was clear and unobstructed, whereas all other seers beheld the truth "through a glass, darkly" (*Yevamot* 49b). For Moses alone, the words of Torah were not just *upon* his heart, but *in* it; they penetrated to the depths of his heart, so that his very being was suffused with the truth of Torah—and nothing else. All the others had Torah *upon* their hearts, not within them. They had no choice but to use analogy and suggestion arising from their imagination, because the whole, unadorned truth eluded them, remaining beyond their capacities of either comprehension or communication.

That is why the Shema uses the term *al levavekha*, "*upon* your heart." For the Torah was given to all the people, not to Moses alone. For them as for us, the penetration of the divine word *into* the heart is an impossibility. Only when we are aided by imagination and by faith can we apprehend the truth that is beyond understanding; for with the exception of Moses, truth is not perceptible without faith, itself an exercise of imagination.

It is this teaching, says R. Zadok, that we glean from the stylistic peculiarity of this expression. Because the human heart is capable of the best and the worst, the divine word does not penetrate it directly. The sacred truth cannot—except for Moses—be perceived by reason alone, but *must be approached with faith and trust as well*—the best that "imagination" has to offer. The Torah, recognizing our human limitations and weaknesses, urges us to aspire to the best of which we are capable: its words of truth shall be placed "*upon* your heart."

Thus is our dilemma resolved. The Torah most certainly intends for us to take this paragraph of the Shema both literally and seriously. We are expected to love God as Scripture's words indicate, and even according to what the Sages saw in them in addition. For though we may consider our religious potential meager, our emotions dilute, and our spiritual capacities thin—and they may indeed be—they are never *too* meager, *too* thin, *too* inadequate to make up in "faith" what we lack in "wisdom." The Torah's truths are applicable at all times and by all individuals. The Torah never makes excessive demands upon us; it merely helps us stretch our capacities. If its words cannot penetrate our very hearts, at least they can rest *upon* our hearts. And that, too, is a magnificent accomplishment.

It is worth adding here another interpretation of "upon your heart" that comes to us by oral tradition from R. Menaḥem Mendel of Kotzk (the one-time teacher of R. Mordecai Joseph Leiner, "the Izhbitzer," who was the master of R. Zadok). The "Kotzker" typically expressed the most psychologically and spiritually profound truths in highly concentrated and sharp aphorisms. Thus, noting the literary oddity in our passage, he had a simple yet potent comment: Even if you feel that your heart is shut tight and words of Torah do not penetrate it—because you are weary or inattentive or preoccupied or simply dull—do not despair. Do not cease your efforts even if you feel that your heart is securely locked against the transcendent message of the divine. Just let the words pile up *upon* your heart. Be confident that in due time your heart will open up, and when it does, inspiration will come. Then, all that has been gathered in, lying patiently *upon* your heart, will tumble *into* your newly opened heart. . . .

This deceptively simple homily, homey yet psychologically compelling, is an important reminder to we who inhabit tumultuous and noisy cities in this frenetic era, that our basic humanity must emerge despite our vast and complex preoccupations, that our shriveled sensitivities and hermetically sealed hearts can and may yet open up, and that it is our responsibility to make that happen—and so allow our lives to be touched by the holy and exalted by the sublime.

Even more, it holds out hope for parents and teachers who may despair over underachieving or unmotivated children. It encourages them to keep on teaching, to wait hopefully for that magic moment when the child's heart will open up, when motivation will take root and a thirst for knowledge will suddenly emerge. At that time, all previous efforts will be vindicated. Thus, whether for ourselves or for our children, the words of Torah should be welcomed *upon* the sealed heart. For nothing will be lost when the heart finally opens to embrace them.

What, if anything, is the relationship between the opening words of the paragraph—"you shall love the Lord your God"—and the second verse: "these words which I command you this day shall be upon your heart"?

The author of the popular medieval work on the 613 commandments, the Ḥinukh,[4] quotes the Sifre, which says:

> It is said, "You shall love the Lord your God" (Deut. 6:4). But (from this) I do not know *how* one loves Him; therefore is it said, "And these words . . . shall be upon your heart" (ibid. 6:6)—as a result of this you will come to know Him by whose word the world came into being.[5]

The Ḥinukh comments:

> That is to say, that by contemplation of the Torah one comes to acknowledge the greatness of the Holy One who is unsurpassed and infinite, and thus will his love for Him be firmly implanted in his heart.

The connection is clear: love for God is enhanced and strengthened by the study of Torah. Thus, to love God fully means to place "these words" upon our hearts.

This passage from Sifre and those who built upon it, such as the *Hinukh,* clearly argue for study of Torah, as opposed to contemplation of Nature, as the major source of love for God—in apparent contradistinction to Maimonides, who, toward the beginning of his great halakhic code, points to Nature as the source of both the love and fear of God.[6] Why this particular stance on the provenance of love?

I suggest that the key to the answer lies in two words at the end of the Sifre passage, two words omitted by the *Hinukh* and others, such as the Mishnah *Berurah.*[7] Those words are *u-medabbek bi'derakhav,* "you will come to know Him by whose word the world came into being *and cling to His ways.*" That is, if we arrive at love for God through contemplating Nature, we may well thereby "come to know Him by whose word the world came into *being.*" What begins with a study of Nature can lead, ultimately, to an appreciation for the Author of Nature *in His role as Creator.* However, such an approach cannot take us beyond that and tell us anything of God's character or personality, of His relationship with the human world. For this we must turn to Torah, which can offer us not only knowledge of the God who created Nature—"by whose word the world came into being"—but *also* of the character of this Deity, "His ways." This latter understanding encourages us to imitate those ways, to "cling" to them and to God. The contemplation of Nature, in contrast, cannot tell us anything about God's ethical character, and it cannot lead to *imitatio Dei;* only the study of Torah can do that. The more *human* way to know God and love Him, according to the Sifre, is through the study of and meditation in Torah.

This linkage between study and love is further amplified in succeeding generations of talmudic authorities and midrashic writers.

The Talmud approvingly records the statement of R. Avdimi, that at the revelation at Sinai, the Holy One raised the mountain over the heads of the assembled Israelites and said to them, "If you accept the Torah, good; if not, here shall be your burial place." The Gemara proceeds to analyze this aggada legally: if the Torah was coerced on us, how can it be considered a valid covenant?

The same quotation of R. Avdimi appears in the Midrash,[8] which does not indulge in halakhic analysis of the validity of the Torah as a binding contract. Instead, it asks another question,[9] the answer to which offers an important distinction as to what aspect of Torah has this power to lead to the love for God. Thus:

Now, if you will say that He raised the mountain over [the Israelites] concerning the Written Torah (i.e., the Pentateuch), then [we may ask]: did the Jews not immediately respond when He asked, "Do you accept the Torah?" that "we shall do and we shall obey"—for [the Written Torah] is short and requires no special effort or pain (to study it)? So, it must be that He [coerced them] concerning the Oral Torah (i.e., the whole of what became the Talmud and its vast literature), for it contains the precise manner of performing the mitzvot, both the easy and the difficult ones, and [its love] is strong as death and its jealousy as cruel as the grave.[10] For one does not [undertake to] study the Oral Law if He does not love the Holy One with all his heart and all his soul and all his might, as it is written, "And you shall love the Lord your God with all your heart and all your soul and all your might" (Deut. 6:5). And whence do we learn that this "love" implies study? See what is written [immediately] afterwards: "And these words . . . shall be upon your heart" (Deut. 6:6). And what kind of study can be said to be "upon your heart?" Read further: "And you shall teach them diligently unto your children"—this refers to the study [of Torah] that requires sharpness.[11]

The Midrash then points out that this first paragraph of the Shema contains no mention of earthly reward for the observance of the commandments, in contradistinction to the second paragraph of the Shema, which is replete with such promises of worldly success and security. Moreover, the first paragraph demands that we love God "with all your might," a condition that is not repeated in the second paragraph. The Midrash explains that the second paragraph speaks of obedience to the commandments (and thus presumably refers to study of the Written Law), whereas the first concerns, in addition, study of the Oral Law, "for whoever loves wealth and pleasure cannot study the Oral Law, for it requires much suffering and lack of sleep, and one must wear himself out and wither away over it. That is why its reward is in the world-to-come. . . . "

One senses here the combined complaint and conceit of the Talmudist who suffers not only the pain of self-denial but also the pangs of intellectual creativity. One senses as well as a rather disdainful attitude toward students of Scripture as opposed to students of Talmud. Indeed, study of the latter is far more demanding of the analytical and dialectical skills of the student. Most important, however, is the clear message that the whole enterprise of Talmud study would never be undertaken were it not for the student's love for the Author of the Torah. Otherwise, the relentless scholarly struggle and the sacrifice of worldly pleasures would hardly be worthwhile.

"And You Shall Teach Them Diligently to Your Children"

Ve'shinantam, generally translated as "you shall teach them (i.e., the words of the Torah) diligently to your children," derives from a Hebrew word meaning "sharp" or "acute."[12] This diligence characterizes a teacher who seeks not merely to stuff quantities of information into a student's head, but who trains him in the intricacies of reasoning, who teaches him an approach to dialectical thinking, and who introduces him to the joys of intellectual and spiritual activity.[13]

To whom does "your children" refer? Not necessarily to one's own children, maintains the Sifre, but to one's students as well: "Even as one's students are called his children, so is he called their father."[14] Thus, while it is certainly meritorious to teach Torah to one's own children, the mitzvah extends to all Jewish children.

What if we fail to give our children a Jewish education? According to the Zohar, the Shema contains within it, in the form of hints, all of the Ten Commandments.[15] Accordingly, we read elsewhere in the Zohar literature:

> A man must teach his son Torah, as it is written, "and you shall teach them diligently to the children"; and if he does not teach him Torah and mitzvot, it is as if he had made a graven image for him, and he is in violation of "you shall not make a graven image," etc.[16]

Further on in the same text we read that an ignoramus in Jewish tradition is suspect of violating all commandments—not only the "ritual" ones, but the ethical precepts as well, from murder to immorality and idolatry. Hence, not teaching a child Torah is tantamount to making an idol for him.

Furthermore, to raise a child, no matter how lovingly, without exposing him or her to the spiritual wealth of the Torah and the moral discipline of the mitzvot implies that, for this parent, the child is seen as an end in himself: the parent's love for that child exists outside the context of any transcendent good or sacred dimension. In effect, the child himself has become a *pessel* or icon, for to absolutize any person, thing, or value is a form of idolatry. As my late and revered teacher, Rabbi Joseph B. Soloveitchik, often taught, idolatry is more than merely bowing to a graven image. For were idolatry no more than such religious fetishism, the prophets' attacks on Jewish idol worship would be both superfluous and irrelevant for us today. But they are not, because idolatry is far more than the physical act of bowing to and worshiping a statue. Rather, it means placing at the center of our values anything, anyone, any value other than God. Whether it is a graven image, science, pleasure, power, money, or a beloved individual, whatever displaces God from the center of our value system is an act of idolatry. True monotheism means to acknowledge that God is absolute and that all else is relative. If we absolutize the relative, we stand guilty of idolatry. So it is when we love our children without acknowledgment of their Creator, who alone confers value upon human beings and activities.

The historical record detailing how Jews have treated their children, loving and caring for them, has earned them the envy and admiration of the world. Indeed, when it was standard practice in some parts of the ancient world to dispose of unwanted children by exposing them to the elements and abandoning them, Jews eschewed such practices. One who disposed of his children in this way was judged guilty of murder, for children, as human beings, were the property of the Creator; even their parents had no absolute rights over them. But this loving and nurturing attitude has always been tied in with a passion for continuing the Jewish tradition. Thus, to care for one's children means providing them with a truly Jewish education. Without such higher goals, parenting is incomplete.

In reciting and listening—and thereby assenting—to the Shema's message to teach the words of Torah diligently to our children, we reissue in contemporary and indeed timeless fashion our rejection of idolatry. And we can feel more confident that we will continue to be "a wise and understanding people," a "People of the Book," who remain devoted to making intellectual, cultural, and spiritual contributions to all humankind.

"And You Shall Talk of Them . . ."

The antecedent of "them" in this verse refers either to the words of the Shema or those of the Torah in general (as was the case in the previous verse, "and *these words* shall be upon your heart"). The talmudic sources generally assume the former when they are discussing halakhic issues and the latter when they broaden their scope to include aggadic or non-halakhic matters.

Thus, a well-known passage in the Talmud expounds our verse:

> Our Rabbis taught: "of them"—but not in prayer. "And you shall talk of them"—of them you have permission to talk, but not of other matters. R. Aḥa says: "And you shall talk of them"—make them a constant occupation, not something casual. Rava said: one who engages in profane (i.e., idle) talk violates a positive commandment, for it is written, "And you shall talk of them"—but not of other matters. (*Yoma* 19b)

It is not altogether clear what some of these cryptic comments mean. The earliest commentators offer a variety of interpretations.

"'Of them'—but not in prayer." For R. Aḥa, the gaonic author of *Sheliltot,* cited approvingly by Rashi,[17] the Rabbis are here making a technical point: the Shema may, and indeed should, be recited aloud ("talk of them"); not so prayer (specifically the *Amidah,* the central portion of the service), which must be recited softly. For Tosafot, however, this means that the distinction between the Shema and prayer is this: the Shema may be interrupted at certain points to greet a person who inspires either fear or reverence in the worshiper, but prayer must never be interrupted for any kind of "talk," even for reasons of fear or respect.[18]

"'And you shall talk of them'—of them you have permission to talk, but not of other matters." For Rashi, this injunction implies a blanket exclusion of childish talk and idle prattle; only Torah is worthy of our conversation.[19] Rabbenu Ḥananel, however, understands the text as more limited in scope: only Torah—i.e., Talmud and the entire halakhic literature of Torah—may be the source of halakhic decision, not extraneous sources.[20]

"R. Aḥa says: *'And you shall talk of them'—make them a constant occupation, not something casual."* The study of Torah must be established as basic to one's regular program, not treated as a casual matter depending upon circumstances. The Sifre puts it even more radically: "Make them (i.e., the words of Torah) your major and not secondary occupation, so that your 'business' shall be exclusively them and you shall not blend in them other matters. Thus, you shall not say, 'I have studied the wisdom of Israel, now I shall go and study the wisdom of the nations of the world.'"[21]

"Rava said: one who engages in profane (i.e., idle) *talk violates a positive commandment, for it is written, 'And you shall talk of them'—but not of other matters."* This dictum by Rava seems rather severe: if you have nothing to say in the way of

Torah, then you should keep silent altogether. However, R. Nathan of Rome interprets this not as a general proscription of non-Torah conversation, but rather as a specific halakhic rule that *when studying Torah,* one may interrupt his studies only for the Reading of the Shema, but not for idle talk.[22] Much later, the Maharal of Prague cautions us that complete silence and refraining from any social conversation are improper, for this shows contempt for other people. What is banned is purposeless and aimless talk, not practical and useful conversation.[23]

Taken together, these rabbinic interpretations teach us that in the course of our daily lives, particularly in conversation ("talk"), we must accord Torah primacy of place.

"When You Sit in Your House, and When You Walk by the Way, When You Lie Down and When You Rise Up"

Our involvement in the study and life of Torah must not be limited in time; we must at *all times* "talk of them," whether we are sitting, walking, going to sleep, or getting up in the morning. At no time should Torah be absent from our life. How does this principle relate to the central theme of the first paragraph of the Shema, namely, the love for God?

R. Naftali Zevi Yehuda Berlin, "the Netziv," tells us that constant study is the surest path to the love for God. If we will but do as the Torah commands us, and "talk of them when you sit," etc., then we shall fulfill the primary commandment: "you shall love the Lord your God."[24]

But the equation may work equally well in the opposite direction: true love of God expresses itself not only in emotional and rapturous ways, but also in the spiritual and intellectual modes so characteristic of normative Judaism. In the picturesque language of Maimonides:

> What is the proper kind of love?—when one loves God with very powerful, great, and overflowing love such that his soul is bound up in the love for God, and he finds himself constantly thinking about it as if he were love-sick [for a woman] and his mind is never distracted from loving her and thinking about her constantly, whether sitting or standing, whether while eating or drinking. Even greater must be the love for God in the hearts of those who love Him—constantly preoccupied with this love, as we were commanded, "with all your heart and all your soul" (Deut. 6:5). This is what Solomon intended when he said, figuratively, "for I am love-sick" (Song of Songs 2:5); and all of Song of Songs is a parable of this matter.[25]

This halakhah in Maimonides' legal code is then followed by three other halakhot fortifying this view, namely, that love is expressed in the ongoing preoccupation with the beloved, specifically, the study of Torah for its own sake. Thus, because we love God, we wish to dote on Him—and what better way than to study His Torah at all times?

We now turn to analyze the details of our verse. As before, note that when the focus is on the recitation of the Shema as the antecedent of "you shall talk of them," what follows is usually a purely halakhic treatment of the verse; when the antecedent is assumed to be the words of the Torah, we generally encounter a broader exegesis of the text.

"When you sit in your house and when you go by the way." In its halakhic analysis, the Talmud sees in this verse an exclusion: when you sit and walk, that is, when you are engaged in mundane, permissible activities, then you are required to read the Shema; but if you are occupied with obligatory activities,

i.e., the performance of a mitzvah, then you are exempt from reciting the Shema.[26] This expresses the halakhic principle *osek be'mitzvah patur min ha-mitzvah,* that one who is already engaged in performing a mitzvah is excused from other positive mitzvot that may come his way at the same time; hence, for instance, one who is traveling during the festival of Sukkot on a mitzvah mission, such as to study Torah or redeem a captive, need not busy himself with the mitzvah of building and dwelling in a *sukkah.* In regard to reciting the Shema, the Talmud offers the special case of a groom on his wedding night: because his mind is preoccupied with thoughts of his bride and the consummation of their relationship—a mitzvah—he need not recite the Shema that night, for it may be assumed that he will not have proper *kavvanah* in his recitation. Nevertheless, an early authority advocates the reverse point of view: Pseudo-Targum Jonathan, an early translator of Scripture into Aramaic, sees in the words "when you sit in your house" a veiled reference to one building a new home or family, i.e., a groom on his wedding night. Thus, the verse is inclusive rather than exclusionary: it includes the groom in the ranks of those required to read the Shema ("You talk of it") *at all times.*[27]

The Zohar's comment on our verse offers much needed homespun wisdom:

> "When you sit in your house." One should conduct himself in his *house* in a wholesome manner, in a constructive manner, so that the members of his household will learn to conduct themselves serenely and joyously. He should not be overbearing towards members of his household, and all that is done in his house should be done in a proper manner.[28]

"When you lie down and when you rise up." The halakhic issues that arose in connection with this phrase were quite con-

troversial before they were definitively decided. The matter was in contention between the two great "Houses," the House or school of Shammai and that of Hillel. The House of Shammai took the verse literally, thus mandating that the recitation of the Shema in the evening be done in a prone position—"when you *lie down*"—and in the morning while standing—"when you *rise up.*" The House of Hillel disagreed, holding that the Torah was referring to the time of day, not the posture of the worshiper. Thus, the Shema should be recited in the evening when people usually go to bed and in the morning when they usually rise.[29] R. Tarfon (who flourished during the first century, when the controversies between the Houses were being decided) relates that he was traveling and, when the time came for him to read the Shema, he lay down, whereupon he was attacked by a gang of robbers, who endangered his life. His colleagues commented that it served him right, for he followed the House of Shammai when the halakha is decided according to the House of Hillel.[30]

But if indeed the Hillelites were right, that the terms "when you lie down" and "when you rise up" refer to evening and morning, respectively, why then did the Torah not say so explicitly—"you shall talk of them . . . in the evening and in the morning?" Why the circumlocution of *lying down* and *rising up?*

An insightful answer is provided by R. Zadok Hakohen of Lublin. According to him, "evening" and "morning" refer to the natural world; they are astronomical terms, with no special relevance to human beings. Thus, were the Torah to specify "evening" and "morning," we might have interpreted the conjunction *vav* as meaning "or" rather than "and," and we would have deduced that it is sufficient to recite the Shema, the acceptance of the "yoke of the Kingdom of Heaven," only once a day. But since the Torah speaks explicitly of going to sleep *and* (the letter *vav*) getting up, speaking in human terms, we know that we are commanded to recite the Shema twice during the course of our day.[31]

For human beings, day and night are qualitatively and functionally different. Upon rising in the morning, we face a workday; when we go to sleep, we are ready for rest, for physical and mental refreshment. Hence, in the morning, we need to recite the Shema and accept upon ourselves the "yoke of the Kingdom of Heaven" so that we succeed in dedicating our varied activities of the day "for the sake of Heaven." That is, we pray that our mundane work, whatever its nature, be impregnated with higher meaning, that it fit into a transcendental context. We set our intention on purpose, hoping that our major mundane occupations are consonant with our ultimate values.

However, when we retire, facing the quotidian period of sleep and rest, we need a different affirmation that we are submitting ourselves to the yoke of Heaven. Here our need to recite the Shema is more subtle: for even when lying in bed and preparing for sleep, a person must know "before Whom he lies."[32] This is a far more difficult task, for it is easier to focus an action than to dedicate a period of rest and physical inactivity to a higher end.

"And You Shall Bind Them for a Sign upon Your Hand and They Shall Be as Frontlets Between Your Eyes"

The first paragraph of the Shema concludes with two "practical" or ritual mitzvot, those of *tefillin* and *mezuzah*. The above verse refers to the first of these mitzvot, the *tefillin* of hand and head.

Contained in the cubic boxes of the *tefillin* are four biblical passages in which the mitzvah of *tefillin* is mentioned. The *tefillin* were originally meant to be worn all day as "signs" that we dedicate heart and hand, principle and practice, to the Creator. However, because the Halakha requires exemplary purity of mind and body during the time one wears the *tefillin,* a practice that proved exceedingly difficult for the average Jew, the mitzvah was eventually restricted to the time of the daily morning service (since *tefillin* are not to be worn at night), especially during the recitation of the Shema and the *Amidah,* particularly the former.

The laws relating to *tefillin* are far too numerous and too detailed to be elaborated here. Nor does the scope of this volume allow for a discussion of the considerable literature concernng the larger meaning of this mitzvah. Let it suffice to cite the eloquent if hortatory passage from the nineteenth-century rabbi and thinker, Rabbi Samson Raphael Hirsch:

> The mind which you dedicate to God through the *tefillin* cannot become the abode of lies, deceit, cunning, and malice. The heart which you sanctify to God through the *tefillin* cannot shrivel into self-seeking or become debased with pleasure-seeking. It must open up to an all-embracing love and dedicate itself in purity to the temple of the All-holy. And, finally, the hand which you have sanctified through the *tefillin* as an instrument for serving God in your actions—can you stretch it out in treachery to the happiness and peace of a brother?[33]

In this passage, Hirsch emphasizes the "all-embracing love" of God. The *tefillin* are a "sign" of that love; they are at one and the same time a reflection of our love for God and a reminder to nourish that love ever more. Hand and head, body and soul, are both dedicated to the love of the One Creator.

This element of love is further emphasized by a distinguished grandson of Rabbi Hirsch. Rabbi Isaac Breuer writes that the *tefillin* renew daily the "covenant of love" between God and

Israel. Indeed, the verse that is recited from the prophet Hosea (2:21–22) as the leather strap of the hand-tefillin is wrapped about the fingers gives elegant expression to that love:

> And I will betroth you unto Me forever; and I will betroth you unto Me in righteousness and in judgment and in loving-kindness and in mercy; and I will betroth you unto Me in faithfulness, and you shall know the Lord.

It is this "betrothal," this "covenant of love" dedicated to the noblest values and highest ideals known to humankind, that finds expression in the *tefillin* that we bind to our limb of action and organ of contemplation.[34]

"And You Shall Write Them upon the Posts of Your House and upon Your Gates"

We now come to the concluding passage of the first paragraph of the Shema, which deals with the second of the two "practical" or ceremonial mitzvot singled out for mention in the Shema. This verse refers to the parchment bearing the first two paragraphs of the Shema, which is wrapped in a small case and affixed to the right doorpost (as one enters the room). (In common parlance, this small scroll, and sometimes its casing as well, is referred to as the *mezuzah*. In the language of Scripture, however, it is the *doorpost* itself that is called the *mezuzah;* there is no special name for the scroll. Nevertheless, already in ancient times the name *"mezuzah"* was borrowed from the doorpost and applied to the scroll containing the Shema.)

The principle behind the mitzvah of *mezuzah* is essentially the same as that for *tefillin:* it is a sign of our love for God. But whereas *tefillin* applies to the personal self, the individual *qua* individual, the mitzvah of *mezuzah* applies to our home—our family and, by extension, our community, city, and country. The belief in the absolute unity of God and the consequent command to love Him are incumbent upon the Jew in all the concentric circles that define his daily existence and endeavor. Not only must the *mezuzah* be affixed to "the posts of your house" but, equally, "upon your gates." The latter term comprises all forms of domicile: "whether it be the gates of court-yards or the gates of alley-ways or the gates of towns and cities—all are required to have a *mezuzah* affixed to them," writes Maimonides in his halakhic code. Regarding the purpose of the mitzvah, Maimonides continues: "whenever he comes in or goes out, he will encounter the unity of the Name of the Holy One, and he will recall his love for Him and bestir himself from his slumber and his idle thoughts about his temporal vanities; and he will know that nothing endures forever and ever, save the knowledge of the Rock of Ages. Thus, he will regain his senses and go in the way of the righteous."[35] Here again, as in the case of *tefillin,* Maimonides emphasizes the love for God as a leitmotif of *mezuzah.*

It is interesting to note that in Maimonides' halakhic *magnum opus,* divided into fourteen separate "books," the second book, *Sefer Ahavah,* "The Book of Love," begins with the Laws of the Shema. It then continues with the Laws of Prayer, *Tefillin, Mezuzah,* the Scroll of the Torah, the *Tzitzit,* the Blessings, and Circumcision. All of these, in one way or another, are intimately connected to the *Grundprinzip* of the love for God.

Thus we find that the whole of the first paragraph of the Shema—from the proclamation of God's unity through the commandment to love Him and, finally, to the mitzvot of *tefillin* and *mezuzah*—form one cohesive whole.

It is fitting to conclude with the following passage from the *Tzeror ha-Mor* by R. Abraham Seba, words that assume even greater significance and pathos when one takes into account the unspeakable suffering and profound human tragedies that befell him when, with so many other Iberian Jews, he was forced into exile during the Expulsion from Portugal in 1492:

> The Torah considered the future—the suffering and the evil which would be decreed against Israel, forcing them to abandon their religion and to abstain from the study of Torah. This is what happened in the Expulsion from Portugal when it was forbidden to preach publicly and to teach children [Torah]. All books and synagogues were taken away, so that we would neither pray nor teach our children. As a result, Torah was all but forgotten by Jews— for how shall we teach our children without books or teachers?
>
> Nothing was left to us save to teach them the Shema— that the Lord is One, and that one ought to love Him and be prepared to die for Him in martyrdom.
>
> Therefore did God give Israel, for such times, this short passage of the Shema which contains (the essence of) the whole of Torah; and if they cannot know the entire passage (i.e., all three paragraphs) at least they will know the one verse *Shema Yisrael* which contains, in the main, the belief in the unity of God. Thus, they may teach this verse to their children so that they know that He is one and He is all-powerful. And if villains should come to coerce them to forsake their God, they should learn to offer their lives up for Him and die in martyrdom. This is what is meant [by the commandment] to love Him "with all your heart and all your soul and all your might."[36]

A Halakhic Analysis
of the Shema

The fundamental halakhic concerns in the matter of the Reading of the Shema are the nature of the mitzvah commandment to recite the Shema; what is included in this mitzvah; how much of the obligatory verses or sections require *kavvanah* such that the failure to achieve such minimal intention renders the whole recitation meaningless and requires repetition with the proper *kavvanah;* and the relation, if any, between the mitzvah of recitation *(keriah)*[1] of the Shema and that of belief in the unity of God.

Nature of the Commandment

The Talmud records a major controversy as to whether the mitzvah of reciting the Shema carries biblical or rabbinic weight.[2] The majority opinion holds that it is biblical, one of the 613 commandments, and hence of primary importance. Such is the decision of the Rishonim (the great medieval Talmudists) such as Maimonides (Rambam), R. Isaac Alfasi (Rif), R. Asher (Rosh), and others. This decision is recorded and confirmed in the *Shulḥan Arukh,* the standard code of Jewish law.[3] The source is cited as a verse of the Shema itself: "and you shall teach them diligently to your children and you shall speak of them when you sit in your house," etc.

R. Yonah Gerondi goes even further in underlining the biblical warrant for the Shema, claiming universal consent for his thesis that the Shema is biblically mandated. He maintains that even the talmudic opinion that the Reading of the Shema is only rabbinic agrees that the *obligation to recite scriptural verses twice a day* ("when you lie down and when you rise up") is truly biblical; what is rabbinic is the choice of *which* verses or sections to recite. In other words, the talmudic expression "the Reading of the Shema is rabbinic" refers not to origin or level of obligation, but to the specific passages designated to be recited rather than other scriptural passages.

What Is Included in the Shema

It is indisputably accepted that the readings required are, first, Deuteronomy 6:4–9 (the first verse of which begins with the word *Shema*), which speaks of the unity of God and the duty to love Him, to speak these words constantly, to teach them diligently to our children, to bind them on hand and on head (the *tefillin*), and to inscribe them on our doorposts (the *mezuzah*). The second section speaks of divine reward and punishment for our observance or neglect of the Torah's commandments and consists of Deuteronomy 11:13–21. The third paragraph is Numbers 15:37–41, which commands that fringes be worn on four-cornered garments (the *tzitzit* on the *tallit*) and, significantly, concludes with a reminder that it is the Lord who took Israel out of Egypt in order to serve Him.

Does the biblical commandment to recite the Shema cover all this scriptural material or only parts of it? There are three opinions among the Rishonim. R. Solomon b. Adret (Rashba) and others confine the biblical obligation to reciting the first verse alone: the Shema itself. According to this opinion, all the rest is rabbinic and hence of secondary importance relative to that first verse of the first section. Rashi, however, holds that the entire first paragraph is biblical.[4] And Rambam appears to include all three paragraphs in the biblical mitzvah.[5]

The Requirement of Kavvanah

How many of these readings require *kavvanah?* To begin *(le'khat'ḥilah),* one must avoid any distractions and intend what he recites throughout all these readings. But what of *be'di'avad,* if one read them but paid no attention: must he repeat them or is he, in such a situation, excused from repeating them and regarded as if he had fulfilled this mitzvah?

The Talmud records three opinions of the Tannaim. R. Akiva maintains that the entire first section, but not the other two, requires *kavvanah*. R. Eliezer restricts the requirement to the first two verses of the first paragraph, and R. Meir—to the first verse, that of the Shema alone.[6]

What is the underlying rationale of these various points of view? My revered teacher, Rabbi Joseph B. Soloveitchik, o.b.m., offers the following interpretation:[7] Rambam explains the Talmud's order of the three sections and the priority given to the first by underscoring the larger themes of the first section, that of the Shema. "The portion of *Shema* is recited first," he writes, "because it contains [the themes of] the unity of God ('the Lord is One'), His love ('you shall love the Lord your God'), and the study of Torah ('you shall teach them,' etc.), which is the great principle upon which all else depends."[8] The second paragraph speaks of all the other commandments of the Torah, as does the third, which mentions, in addition, the exodus from Egypt. These three principles implicit in the Shema section are the major constituents of *kabbalat 'ol malkhut shamayim*, the submission to the yoke of the Kingdom of Heaven, which is the essence of the Shema.

This interpretation throws light on the tannaitic dispute as to how far we go in demanding *kavvanah*. R. Akiva is the most straightforward in insisting upon *kavvanah* for the complete first portion of the Shema; after all, the third of these principles, the study of Torah, appears in the *fourth* verse of the first section, and it makes eminently good sense to require *kavvanah* for more than the first verse or two. Hence, one must exercise *kavvanah* for the entire first section. The other two opinions, however, remain problematic. Rabbi Soloveitchik's response is that R. Eliezer must hold that the two central themes of unity and love are sufficient to qualify as "accepting the yoke of the Kingdom of Heaven," and therefore it is adequate to achieve *kavvanah* for the first two verses, which reflect these themes. By the same token, R. Meir must consider the theme of the unity of God of such overarching importance that attention paid to this one verse of the Shema qualifies as "accepting the yoke of the Kingdom of Heaven" and thus as having recited the Shema with the minimum necessary intention. Moreover, by having *kavvanah* for only part of the first paragraph—the two verses for R. Eliezer and the first for R. Meir—and thereby succeeding to *kabbalat 'ol malkhut shamayim*, one fulfills the requirement of affirming all three principles, perhaps because the lesser are somehow implied in the larger principles, which are not only more fundamental but also more comprehensive.

Now, while this pattern is structurally attractive and rings true, it remains to be explained why, according to R. Eliezer and R. Meir, the first or first two principles imply the remaining themes. How, for instance, does the unity of God include, according to R. Meir, the love of God and the study of Torah?

I venture the following amplification of Rabbi Soloveitchik's thesis: It is not that the earlier principle or principles *imply* the latter, but that they *lead* to them. Thus, R. Eliezer will hold that if one affirms the unity and love for God, this will invariably lead him to the study of Torah. More than a millennium after R. Eliezer, Rambam defined the love of God as inextricably bound up with the knowledge of God (see chapter 10); the same holds true for the very closely related commandment to study the Torah. For R. Meir, unity implies love (see chapter 6) and, hence, at one remove, the study of Torah as well.

Recitation and Belief

From a purely formal halakhic point of view, how many separate mitzvot or biblical commandments does one fulfill when reciting that first verse of the Shema with full *kavvanah?*

It appears that there are three such distinct mitzvot that are performed in the process of reciting the Shema. The first, which is interesting but need not concern us here, is that of *talmud torah,* the study of Torah; "You shall teach them diligently to your children" implies both the study and the teaching of Torah. Reciting the verse *Shema Yisrael* is certainly no less an act of the study of Torah than the reading of any other scriptural verse.

The two other mitzvot that are of more immediate concern to us are the mitzvah of *keriah,* reading or reciting of the Shema, and the mitzvah of *yihud Hashem,* affirming the unity of God. Evidence of the essentially distinct nature of these two may be adduced from the classification adopted by Rambam. In his great halakhic code, the *Mishneh Torah,* he codifies the laws of *keriah* in his *Hilkhot Keriat Shema,* the "Laws of the Reading of the Shema"; but the commandment to believe or affirm divine unity is treated by him in *Hilkhot Yesodei ha-Torah,* "Laws of the Foundations of the Torah." Moreover, in his earlier work on the 613 commandments, he identifies the affirmation of divine unity as the second positive commandment and the Reading of the Shema as the tenth. Hence, the mitzvah of *yiḥud Hashem* is not dependent upon that of *keriat Shema*. The Rabbis, however, identified the reading of this verse as the opportune moment to fulfill as well the commandment to affirm faith in the unity of God. Hence, the act of reading the Shema with proper *kavvanah* entails the performance of two commandments, that of *keriah* and that of *yiḥud Hashem* (in addition, as mentioned above, to that of *talmud torah*).

The differences between the two are clear and practical. The commandment to affirm divine unity is unlimited; it applies to all times and places and obligates men and women equally. The mitzvah to read the Shema is limited to twice a day ("when you lie down and when you rise up") and, because it is confined to specific times, obligates only men and not women; the latter are required to observe only positive commandments that are not time-bound in addition to (almost) all negative ("You shall not") commandments.[9] Moreover, the Reading of the Shema is a physical, externalized act and therefore requires a preceding benediction.[10] The mitzvah of *yiḥud Hashem,* however, is nonphysical. It is an internal thought process and therefore requires no initial blessing.

There is yet a third difference, and that entails a significant insight into the nature of the *kavvanah* required for reading the Shema. This revolves around the question: How does this *kavvanah* relate to the *kavvanah* prescribed for all other positive commandments of the Torah, such as the eating of matzah on Passover or laying the *tefillin* every weekday?

Ramban declares that there is no substantial difference between them. In all cases, including that of the Shema, one must intend minimally only the readiness to perform a mitzvah.

When the Talmud speaks of *mitzvot tzerikhot kavvanah*, that the act of the mitzvah must be accompanied by *kavvanah*, it refers exclusively to the awareness that we thereby fulfill an obligation placed upon us by our Creator. Nothing more detailed, specific, or sophisticated is necessary—and that holds true for the Shema as it does for all other commandments of the Torah.

Rashba, however, disagrees and maintains that, unlike other commandments that relate to purely physical acts, the mitzvah of recitation lies somewhere between a mere physical act and one of thinking or mentation. Hence, the *kavvanah* required for the Shema is that of understanding the meaning of the words one speaks. Intending only to perform an obligatory mitzvah is inadequate in such a case and does not therefore qualify as the minimum *kavvanah* for the Shema. (Rambam, according to most later authorities, agrees with Rashba, although this interpretation of Rambam is not unanimous.)

Now, according to Ramban, the *kavvanah* to fulfill an obligation combines with the physical act of articulation; together, the mitzvah has been properly performed. This, however, is confined to the mitzvah of *reading* the Shema. Not so with regard to the mitzvah of *yiḥud Hashem*: this is a totally abstract experience, essentially unconnected with any physical act, even that of articulation. (Its relation to the Reading of the Shema is accidental, not essential, as mentioned above.) Hence, there must be *kavvanah* of the full content of the mitzvah, i.e., the personal and unconditional affirmation of divine unity. Without this particular *kavvanah*, nothing has been accomplished; there is no physical act involved, and if there is no intention to affirm divine unity, there is nothing at all to qualify as a separate and distinct act. The full *kavvanah* or meditation of *yiḥud Hashem* is the equivalent of the act of merely eating the matzah in that Passover-related commandment. Hence, the less

demanding *kavvanah* to fulfill an obligation is utterly insuffi-
cient in the case of the mitzvah of *yiḥud Hashem*—which
requires *meditation* rather than simple intention to perform a
mitzvah.

Here then is yet another difference between the commandment to read the Shema and that of the affirmation of divine
unity. The former requires no *kavvanah* as to the content
of what is being recited, only the awareness that by this recitation one fulfills a mitzvah. Indeed, the talmudic ruling that
be'di'avad, post factum, one has achieved the mitzvah even
without *kavvanah,* means that if we had no intention at all, but
simply read the Shema as a matter of habit, we need not repeat
the recitation if and when we later realize that we were merely
mumbling words without meaning. The case of *yiḥud Hashem,*
however, is totally different. Here neither a generalized intention to fulfill a technical commandment nor an appreciation of
the simple meaning of the words recited is adequate. In the
absence of a specific awareness of the *content* of the mitzvah,
without a fully conscious affirmation of the unity of God, we
have done nothing at all and must repeat the mitzvah in order
to perform it properly.[11]

Notes

Chapter 1

1. See, in detail, chapter 16.
2. Adina Blady Szwajger, *I Remembered Nothing More,* trans. T. Darowska and D. Stok (New York: Wm. Collins & Co., 1990), p. 45.
3. The incident is mentioned in the memoirs of Jacob Freimark of Suwalki, preserved in Yad Vashem, #03/2270. I am grateful to Prof. Tzipora Weiss-Halivni for bringing it to my attention.
4. Yaffa Eliach Collection, Center for Holocaust Studies, Museum of Jewish Heritage, New York.
5. See the *Jerusalem Report,* July 11, 1996, p. 16.
6. The origin of this recitation is, according to *Teshuvot ha-Geonim,* the banning by the Persian King Yazdegerd (438–457) of the public reading of the Shema. The fifth-century Amora, R. Naḥman bar Huna, therefore decreed that it be recited before the beginning of the regular service.
7. Thus, Maimonides, under attack for not elaborating upon the belief in the resurrection of the dead, defended himself by pointing to this precedent, i.e., the solitary occasion the Torah mentions monotheism as a commandment (in the Shema), despite its centrality in Judaism; see his *Treatise on Resurrection,* ed. Joshua Finkel (New York: American Academy for Jewish Research, 1939), p. 19.
8. This passage is rather exceptional in that it expresses no preference for *naaseh* over *nishma.* The conventional view in rabbinic literature emphasizes the supremacy of deed and conduct

(*naaseh,* we will do), over *nishma,* which means not only "hear" and "obey" but also "understand"; thus, the aggada of the angels amazed at how the Children of Israel learned this high principle of the priority of conduct to full understanding—"who revealed to them this secret?" *(mi gilah raz zeh le'vanai).* Our midrash apparently reverses the order of importance. So too R. Saadia Gaon, in his commentary on the Torah (Kapah edition, Jerusalem: 1962) on this verse, changes the sequence. Indeed, the Torah itself elsewhere reverses the order; see Deut. 5:24. See too the interesting and original comment by Rabbi Moshe Shmuel Glasner to *Ki Tissa* (*Shevivei Esh* [Des: 1903]), who accepts the more popular interpretation of *nishma* as "we will understand" and attributes this preference for behavior over understanding to the slave mentality of the newly emancipated Israelites, something to which Moses vigorously objected. Unquestionably, Judaism places exceedingly high value on action and deed; practice is a hallmark of Jewish devotion. Even without midrashic sources, it is obviously a distinguishing characteristic of halakhic Judaism. Yet there are other opinions—and our midrash apparently is one of them—that should not be neglected in assessing the balance between thought and deed, idea and action.

9. *Shulḥan Arukh, Oraḥ Ḥayyim,* 98:2 and 101, and cf. *Hagahot Maimuniyot* to Maimonides, *Hilkhot Tefillah,* 4. See too my *Halakhot ve'Halikhot* (Jerusalem: Mosad Harav Kook, 1990), chapter 6.

10. The demand for *kavvanah* is even more emphatic in the Kabbalah than in the Halakha. While there is also a change in definition—the halakhic understanding of *kavvanah* is that of the exoteric content of words or deeds, whereas Jewish mysticism, usually using the plural *kavvanot,* adds a heavy overlay of esoteric "mysteries"—the fundamental fact of the need for concentration and thought and not simple mechanical articulation or action is of enormous importance for the Kabbalah. Thus, for instance, the Zohar (III, *Behar,* 108a) offers the following analogy for *kavvanah* in the Shema, which is also known as *kabbalat 'ol malkhut shamayim,* "the acceptance of the yoke of the

Kingdom of Heaven": In order to derive benefit from an ox, one must first place a yoke upon it; without the yoke ('ol), it is of no use. So too the Reading of the Shema is ineffective unless one first submits to the "yoke" of Heaven, i.e., the awareness in reciting the Shema that one thereby submits to the discipline of obedience to God. Thus, the Zohar too gives priority to the Shema over prayer in relation to the obligation of kavvanah.

Chapter 2

1. R. David Cohen, Kol ha-Nevuah (Jerusalem: Mosad Harav Kook, 1970).
2. See R. Yehuda Halevi, Kuzari, 1:89.
3. Rabbi Adolf Altmann, "The Meaning and Soul of 'Hear, O Israel,'" trans. Barbara R. Algin, in Jewish Values in Jungian Psychology, ed. Levi Meier (Lantham, University Press of America: 1991), p. 61.
4. Ibid., p. 62.
5. Ibid., p. 61.
6. Benei Yisasekhar, Adar 3 derush 2; also Sivan, maamar 5, 19.
7. Theodore Roszak, Where the Wasteland Ends (Garden City, N.Y.: Doubleday, 1972), p. 112. I am grateful to Zvi Kolitz for bringing this work to my attention.
8. This holds true primarily for biblical Hebrew. In later, rabbinic Hebrew, "I see" (much like the idiomatic English expression of our own day) implies understanding and even assent, as does "I hear." Thus, in Avot 2:13, 14, "I see the words of Elazar b. Arakh" in the sense of approving his dictum.
9. See supra, n. 1.
10. A similar point is made by Rav Kook (see the Introduction to his 'Olat Re'iyah [Jerusalem: Mosad Harav Kook, 1962] edited by his son R. Zvi Yehuda Kook). Rav Kook held that questions, doubts, and unproven hypotheses have their place in the rest of life, including Halakha, but prayer is a time when the spirit quests and presupposes certainty and clarity. Thus R. Kook explains the apparent contradiction between Maimonides' rul-

ing in his halakhic code and his philosophic disquisition in his *Guide for the Perplexed.* In the former, Maimonides decides, in keeping with talmudic teaching, that in performing the biblical mitzvah of sending away the mother bird when taking the eggs or chicks from the nest, one must not say, "Thy mercies extend to the bird's nest." In the *Guide,* however, Maimonides offers divine concern for the suffering of the inferior species as a reason for this very mitzvah. R. Kook affirms the legitimacy of seeking a rational explanation of the commandments, in this case divine compassion; but since this is only conjecture, because the reason is not mentioned explicitly in the Torah, it cannot be incorporated in *prayer,* which is what the Talmud had in mind and which Maimonides codified as halakha.

11. This is not the place to expand on the theme of religious doubt. I have elsewhere attempted to show that the honest doubter need not feel excluded from the community of the faithful and have offered some guidance in how to orient one's self to doubt when one encounters it (*Faith and Doubt* [New York: Ktav Publishing, 1971], chapter 1). Descartes invited the world to doubt everything. "Fortunately," writes Robert Nisbet, "that Cartesian injunction is psychologically impossible, but if it were, we would be cast into a void." According to Christopher Morley, Nisbet continues, de Tocqueville early in life wrote that were he asked to class human miseries, he would so in the following order, "Disease, Death, and Doubt"; but later in life, he altered the order and deliberately declared doubt to be the most insupportable of all evils, worse than death itself (*Prejudices: A Philosophical Dictionary* [Cambridge: Harvard University Press, 1982], pp. 92–3).

12. R. Zadok Hakohen of Lublin, in his *Dover Zaddik.*

Chapter 3

1. See Israel Eldad, *Hegyonot ha-Mikra* (Jerusalem: Sulam, 1959), p. 241.

2. Normally the name "Jacob" is used for him personally as the (third) father of the Jewish people. However, the name "Israel" is sometimes used for Jacob himself, in his capacity as father of his people, as in 1 Chron. 29:10—"Wherefore David blessed the Lord before all the congregation, and David said 'blessed be You, Lord the God of *Israel our father,* for ever and ever.'" Our midrash is, therefore, not too far from the *peshat* or plain meaning of the text in identifying him as the "Israel" of the Shema.

3. Note that according to this midrash, the recitation of *Barukh shem kevod* was done quietly by Jacob himself and is not a compromise proposed by the Rabbis to resolve the dilemma of offending the memory of either Jacob or Moses, as the parallel text in the Talmud would have it.

4. Sifre to Deuteronomy, *piska* 31.

5. Whether this aggada is a legend woven around the historical figure of Jacob, suggested by the name "Israel," or a tradition of which Moses was aware and handed down with other oral traditions at Sinai, is irrelevant. Even if the former, it is a most valid insight into the nature of this grand profession of monotheistic faith, integrating the worshiper into the sublime continuum of Jewish *emunah,* the faith of Israel. Netziv (R. Naftali Zevi Yehuda Berlin) in his *Ha'amek Davar* to Deut. 6:4 answers the question of Ramban why the Torah here uses the first person plural possessive, "*our* God," rather than "*your* God," which occurs in all other verses preceded by the invocation, "Hear O Israel": Moses knew of this tradition of Jacob and his sons and referred to it specifically. The possessive "*our*" is thus critical. Support for this interpretation may be found in *Targum* Jonathan b. Uziel to Deut. 6:5, where the second verse of the Shema, "You shall love," etc., is prefaced with the words, "The Prophet Moses said to the people, the House of Israel." In other words, the second verse is explicitly attributed to Moses, to emphasize that the first "Hear O Israel" was uttered by Jacob, and Moses only repeated the phrase in his talk to his people and later committed it to writing in the Torah. Netziv avers that this is but one

of a number of cases of oral traditions that were incorporated, in whole or in part, by Moses into the (Written) Torah.

Chapter 4

1. The difference in the usage of these two Names forms the basis of the documentary hypothesis and the "Higher Criticism" of the Bible, as is well known. Jewish exegetes solved the problem by the general rule that *Elohim* represents stern divine judgment, while *Hashem* symbolizes divine mercy and love. The Rabbis were fully aware of those cases where this rule apparently does not apply, and they almost invariably explained such exceptions. We here shall follow this rabbinic tradition.

2. This duality of the natural and the historical is anticipated in the *birkhot keriat shema,* the two major benedictions preceding the reading of the Shema in both the morning and evening services. The first of these blessings describes the divine governance of the natural order in all its splendor. The second concerns God's role in history—the choosing of Israel, the love for Israel, the continuum of the generations under God's rule—and, above all, the giving of the Torah at Sinai for constant study by Israel.

3. Maimonides defines *tov* in the scriptural context, as the realization of the divine will for the sake of the particular object so described, rather than as a means to some other created object; *Guide for the Perplexed,* 3:13.

4. R. Yaakov Zevi Mecklenburg, in his *Ha-Ketav ve'ha-Kabbalah,* tries to synthesize these two dimensions of *tov.* For him, it signifies not that the creation was good—as if God were an artist stepping back in self-congratulating appreciation of his handiwork—but an explanation of *why* the Creator created, namely, because *He* (God) is good. This is based on the retranslation of *va-yera* not as "He saw," but as "He brought into being." Although, he maintains, the usual translation is "he saw," the form of the verb is unusual—*hif'il,* causative—and therefore legitimately lends itself to "he made visible" or "he brought into being." The effort, while admirable, is not totally successful.

God's *tov* as overflowing love, *ḥesed* or the effluence of "giving-
ness," is still metaphysical and not necessarily moral or person-
alistic. See my *The Good Society: Jewish Ethics in Action* (New
York: Viking Press, 1974), pp. 3–9.

5. The tendency of primitive man to personalize the forces of
Nature, and his internal drives as well, conceiving of them as
independent and autonomous powers that he then apotheosized,
comes to mind as we read of the rash of psychiatric cases of
"multiple personalities" that have attracted public attention in
recent years. It is a psychological illustration of the dangers of
absolutizing the relative (which is really what idolatry is all
about) in a pathological manner. In an ironic revival of the "possessions" and exorcisms of our recent superstitious past—the
phenomenon of "the dybbuk" comes to mind—psychiatrists
have identified more and more cases of people who not only
develop different facets of personality (we all do that) but trans-
form them into independent personalities which inhabit their
body. (I am indebted to my son Joshua, which has been profes-
sionally involved with a number of such cases, for the information on the psychiatry of multiple personalities.) These "persons" are not a matter of metaphor or rhetoric; they are
experienced by the patient as very real indeed. A patient may
have a large number of such separate personalities inhabiting
his—usually her—body and often be only dimly or sporadically
or not at all aware of some or all of them. Like the gods who
populated the theological universe of the ancient pagans, these
personalities may form alliances with each other, strive with each
other, and indeed often attempt to harm and even kill each
other—and sometimes succeed, and the patient is lost. Though
we are not in possession of an adequate scientific explanation for
this phenomenon, it appears that the human mind proves to be
a wonderful, awe-inspiring entity as it helps the individual sur-
vive inhuman assaults on the vulnerable ego by personalizing
the various forces in life, both friendly and hostile, and conceiving of them as different people—with different names, gen-
ders, voices, handwriting, dispositions, etc. The old phylogeny-

ontogeny scheme that used to be popular in embryology—that the developing human foetus and the evolution of the species parallel each other—seems to find its analogue here: the patient exhibits the psychiatric equivalent of the underlying theology of the primitive religions of mankind. The equation reads the other way as well: the tendency toward pagan dualism is the theological equivalent of the very serious disease called multiple personality disorder. And if so, manifestations of such dualism in our contemporary lives may also be understood as invalid and unauthentic responses to the pressures and threats of the world about us. To retain both our spiritual integrity and our mental health, it is important for us to recognize and affirm, regularly, that the various personalities we assume for different times and occasions are but masks we put on or take off in a socially acceptable manner (indeed, the word *personality* derives from the *persona* or mask that actors would don to represent different roles in the early history of drama); that the joys of life and its frustrations and disappointments, the bliss and the grief, are not merely chance events that buffet us arbitrarily, but that they, and all life, issue from one Source and are thus ultimately coherent. It is the limited native intelligence of our species that does not permit us to fully comprehend the details of that coherence. But it objectively exists. And it is this unifying coherence, originating in the oneness of existence itself, and the awareness that such oneness indeed exists that make life meaningful and valuable.

6. This passage does not appear in the Babylonian Talmud, for which reason some authorities deduce that the two Talmuds are in disagreement with each other. But whether the Babylonian Talmud does or does not agree with the Jerusalem Talmud, it is clear that the latter considers the Tetragrammaton as implying divine sovereignty and lordship of the world; were it not so, the entire interpretation would be meaningless. See R. Joseph Babad, *Kometz Minḥah*, the addendum to his *Minḥat Ḥinukh*, 420.

Chapter 5

1. However, the ascription of this hope for the future to Micah is forced; there is more than a bit of an apologetic strain in this interpretation, which would introduce embryonic contemporary notions of mutual tolerance and religious pluralism into antiquity. The prophet obviously speaks in defiant terms: we will march under the banner of the One God even if the rest of the world continues to maintain its various forms of paganism. Zephaniah, in the verse quoted by Rashi, is quite clear; he insists upon an unambiguous commitment to the Jewish conception of the unity of God by the nations of the world.

2. Menachem Kellner, "A Suggestion Concerning Maimonides' 'Thirteen Principles' and the Status of Non-Jews in the Messianic Era," in *Tura: Oranim Studies in Jewish Thought*, vol. 1 (Tel Aviv: Ha-kibbutz ha-Meuḥad, 1988), pp. 249–60; and his *Maimonides on Judaism and the Jewish People* (Albany: SUNY Press, 1991), pp. 33–48. See too his "Chosenness, Not Chauvinism," in *A People Apart*, ed. Daniel H. Frank (Albany: SUNY Press, 1993), pp. 55–6.

3. Indeed, there are several other places in his halakhic code, the *Mishneh Torah*, in which Maimonides uses this locution in referring to Judaism. There may thus be some merit to this claim, even though the entire passage is not without its difficulties (especially the use of the verb "they will *return*").

4. See chapter 15 for an elaboration on the theme of the "dependency" of God on man.

5. See his *Gevurot Hashem*, chapter 47; and *Derush al ha-Torah*, p. 27a. From Maharal, the expression flourished, especially in hasidic literature. The first source is probably *Tikkunei Zohar*, 21, p. 60b: "there is no king without a kingdom."

6. One of the very earliest of the famous Spanish Jewish philosophers, the saintly R. Baḥya, concludes in the first part *(shaar ha-yiḥud)* of his *Ḥovot ha-Levavot* ("Duties of the Heart") that it is a mitzvah to reflect on the unity of God and, moreover, *to instruct the pagans in this doctrine*. Thus, in his third chapter,

NOTES TO PAGES 35-40

R. Baḥya, commenting on the verse in Deut. 4:6, "for this is your wisdom and your understanding in the sight of the peoples," writes: "It is impossible that the [other] nations will acknowledge our wisdom and understanding without us bringing rational proof to the truth of our Torah and our faith."

7. See his *Likkutei Halakhot, Oraḥ Ḥayyim, Hilkhot Keriat Shema, hal. 3,* no. 10.

8. Both these laws are mentioned in *Berakhot* 13a. See chapter 2.

9. See also Rabbi Menachem Mendel Kasher in his *Shema Yisrael* (undated).

10. See chapter 15 for the interpretation of the Kaddish by S. Y. Agnon.

11. This articulates well with what was said above, namely, that the different connotations of "Lord" *(Hashem)* and "God" *(Elohim)* are reflected in the two blessings preceding the Shema, which speak of the creation of nature and the direction of history. If we now accept this eschatological interpretation of the last two words, *Hashem eḥad,* "the Lord is One," then we have as well a reflection of that theme in the third of the three blessings, that which follows the reading of the Shema, namely, the blessing of *geulah,* redemption.

Chapter 6

1. The terms "above and below," according to Rashi, refer to heaven and earth.

2. Rashi, Maimonides, and others consider the whole meditation as one *kavvanah* that should be maintained at the second syllable. *Talmidei* R. Yonah and others (and so codified in the *Shulḥan Arukh*) hold that "above and below" should be meditated at the *ḥet,* and the "four corners" at the *dalet.*

3. *Sefer ha-Yirah,* p. 20. The authorship is generally attributed to R. Yonah, but that has now been questioned by contemporary scholars.

4. On this last clause of R. Yonah, that if one cannot keep in mind the entire meditation of the Talmud he should resort to the Sifre's

interpretation, Rabbi M. M. Kasher in his *Shema Yisrael,* 244, maintains that R. Yonah refers not only to the untutored person as opposed to the scholar, but also to the more knowledgeable person who may feel pressed for time.

5. It appears that Rashi was working with the Alfasi text rather than our printed one. Thus, Rashi uses the words "heaven and earth" in place of "above and below"; the former is the Alfasi reading; the latter, the printed version. More important: Rashi comments, "You have prolonged the period in which you can meditate that the Lord is One in heaven and earth and its four corners." Clearly, we are dealing with a *time* rather than a *content* problem. This may well explain why Rashi, in his commentary on the Torah, offers only the Sifre interpretation and ignores the Talmud's. Quite simply, he read the talmudic passage as referring to the duration of the meditation rather than exclusively to its substance.

6. See, for instance, *Sukkah* 26b and *Baba Kamma* 59b.

7. There is one alternative reading of our text that provides an instructive psychological insight: The Munich Manuscript contains a variant cited also by R. Asher and others, which includes one additional word: *alekha,* i.e., "so that you declare Him king *over yourself* and over heaven," etc. In all probability, the other variants skip the *alekha* because it is comprehended in the universality of "heaven and earth," etc. Yet it deserves emphasis because of a wise insight by the great ethicist R. Israel Salanter, founder of the Musar movement that it is easy enough to intend that He rules over heaven and earth and the four corners of the world, but to make Him king, *alekha,* over yourself—now, that's considerably more difficult. . . .

8. See his *Ayin AYeH* to *Berakhot* 13b.

9. There may have been a strong influence by the Maharal on Rav Kook in conceiving this idea. See, e.g., the former's *Tiferet Yisrael,* chapter 19. This play on the number eight is reminiscent, too, of the comment of the Mabit in his *Bet Elohim* that the designation of the eighth day for a child's circumcision is an indication of the elevation of the child from the natural to the super-

natural order as a result of his entry into the Covenant. Also, the Talmud (*Menaḥot* 29b), discussing the proper orthography in the writing of the Torah scroll (and not referring to the Shema), states that scrolls prepared by careful and expert scribes contain a vertical line above the horizontal bar of the letter (exactly what that means was in dispute between Rashi and Rabbenu Tam), which indicates that "He lives in the exalted heights of the world." Perhaps this, too, is a temporal rather than spatial allusion—He lives above the world, i.e., He is timeless, eternal. That passage may well have served as a source for Rav Kook.

10. This last point might possibly be considered debatable because there is a controversy among halakhic authorities as to whether the ten verses recited in each section of the three must conclude with a verse from the Pentateuch or from the Prophets. Hence, the concluding of the section with the Shema may simply be in compliance with the former opinion, rather than an allusion to its eschatological character. In that case, it quite possibly was borrowed from the Rosh Hashanah liturgy and found its way into the daily service. Nevertheless, the likelihood is that the connection between the unity of God and the End of Days is responsible for all three cases; see Kasher, *Shema Yisrael,* p. 245.

11. See his *Judische Schriften,* ed. B. Strauss (Berlin: C. A. Schwetschke, 1924), vol. I, pp. 88–9; and his *Religion of Reason Out of the Sources of Judaism,* trans. S. Kaplan (New York: 1972), p. 45. David Novak ("The Election of Israel: Outline of a Philosophical Analysis," in *A People Apart,* op. cit.) maintains that for Cohen there is a sharp difference between the two terms: *Einzigkeit* refers exclusively to God in His singularity or uniqueness, whereas *Einheit* refers to the unity toward which humanity must aspire.

12. The question as to whether this particular term is effective as a marriage proposal is left unresolved in the Talmud. We therefore consider the marriage as *safek,* or doubtful, applying to it the stringencies of both the single and the married state. See too Rambam, *Hilkhot Ishut,* 3:7 and *Shulḥan Arukh, Even Ha-ezer,* 27:3. That does not affect our point, however, which is not rele-

vant to the technical question in matrimonial law but is based on the stylistic similarity to *meyuḥedet,* which is considered by the Talmud as a proper formulation because it implies, as does *mekudeshet,* the setting aside of an individual for special purposes.

Chapter 7

1. See chapter 3.
2. For a review of most of these definitions—which often, though not always, were motivated by interreligious polemics—see Daniel Lasker, "Definitions of 'One' and Divine Unity," in *Studies in Jewish Thought,* ed. S. O. Heller-Wilenski and M. Idel (Jerusalem: Magnes Press, 1989), pp. 51–61 (Hebrew).
3. I suggest, according to this acosmic thesis, another explanation for the custom of placing the hand over one's eyes upon reciting the Shema—a practice approved in the Talmud in the name of R. Judah; it symbolizes the unreality of the phenomenal world that is perceived by the senses. The eyes are therefore shielded in order to emphasize that the sensate "world" does not in fact exist, that God alone is "real."
4. The Cordoveran dichotomy in a way anticipates the contemporary theory of complementarity—that there are two opposite ways of apprehending the same truth. Thus, light can be conceived of as both undulatory and discrete particles—and the equations work out equally well for both wave phenomena and for discrete quanta; yet both apparently contradictory states are true. See my *Torah Umadda,* (Northvale, N.J. and London: Jason Aronson Inc., 1990), pp. 232–8.
5. On the Ziditchover, see my *The Religious Thought of Hasidism* (Hoboken, N.J.: Ktav Publishing, in progress), chapter I, selection 4, and notes thereto.
6. From *pan-en-theos,* "all is in God" instead of *pantheism,* that "all is God." Pantheism denies any divine existence outside the universe because it identifies Him with the cosmos. Panentheism grants His immanence in the cosmos, and certainly holds Him to

NOTES TO PAGES 54–55

be the Cause of the world and its ontological anchor, but asserts that His existence is not limited to the world. The concept is strikingly similar to the dictum of R. Ami in the Midrash (Genesis Rabbah, 68:9; see too Exodus Rabbah, 45:6 and Tanḥuma to *Ki Tissa*), "He is the place of the world, but the world is not His place."

7. *Tikkunei Zohar, Tikkun,* 1.
8. In kabbalistic language, this yearning is referred to as *mayyim nukvin,* "female waters."
9. In kabbalistic language, *mayyim dukhrin,* "male waters," the divine desire to give—the counterpart of the "female waters," the human desire to receive and be accepted.
10. R. Zvi Hirsch of Ziditchov, in the beginning of his lengthy essay, *Ketav Yosher Divrei Emet,* appended to his *Sur me-Ra va-Aseh Tov.*
11. Thus R. Shneur Zalman, loc. cit., notes that the last word in the traditional verse, *va-ed* ("forever"), is equal to *eḥad,* "one." This "equation" is achieved by certain conventional but unusual ways of translating the Hebrew letters to numerals; in this case, the permissibility of exchanging the letters *vav* and *alef* for each other and so for the letters *'ayin* and *ḥet.* Thus, *va-ed (vav, 'ayin, dalet)* becomes *eḥad (alef, ḥet, dalet).*
12. Hence, for the Ziditchover it is quite legitimate to think of reciting the Shema without necessarily adding immediately the *Barukh shem kevod,* since the two are independent of each other. The tradition concerning Jacob's recital of the *Barukh shem kevod* is a historic coincidence, but that inserted verse has no inherent connection to the Shema verse. For the acosmists, however, the two are intimately linked and of necessity must appear together at every liturgical mention of the Shema. Given this difference between them, the recitation of the Shema verse during the *Kedushah* of the Sabbath *Musaf* service, without the concomitant *Barukh shem kevod,* is understandable according to the Ziditchover but poses a problem of sorts for R. Shneur Zalman and R. Ḥayyim.

NOTES TO PAGES 56–57

13. Max Kadushin has pointed out that in the Talmud, wherever we find ascetic references they are not meant for their own sake as a way of attaining the spiritual by suppressing the corporeal but, rather, for the sake of the study of Torah. See his *Organic Thinking* (New York: Bloch Publishing, 1938), pp. 53–7.

14. *Tzidkat ha-Tzaddik*, 154.

15. Thus, Rabbi Avraham Chanoch Glitzenstein (*Or ha-Ḥasidut* [Brooklyn: Kehat Otzar Hachasidim, 1965], p. 34f) regards the standard, i.e., non-acosmic, view as heresy. But how can one regard as heretical that which so many generations before the end of the eighteenth century accepted as genuine Jewish doctrine? The all-too-easy answer offered is that novel interpretations of the Oral Law obligate only the future, not the past; for just as in strictly halakhic matters once a ruling is universally accepted, all other views remain outside the pale of Halakha, so with regard to theological issues, specifically those that were "revealed" in Hasidism.

16. I have not seen any serious halakhic discussion on these divergent interpretations of the single most fundamental verse in the Torah, nor is this the place for a comprehensive treatment of the subject. While it is possible to find indirect halakhic indications to support the acosmic interpretation and its incorporation in the meditation on the Shema, there is also evidence for the reverse view. As one example, there appears to be one source where such an inclination can be deduced, although without coming to any definitive judgment on the matter, and that is the Shema recited *before* the morning service as part of a passage that comes in large part from *Tanna de'vei Eliyahu*. Here we recite: ". . . Happy are we, how goodly is our portion, how pleasant our lot, and how happy our heritage! Happy are we who, early and late, morning and evening, twice every day, declare," and then follows the verse *Shema Yisrael*, etc. Some prayer books follow this with the *Barukh shem kevod* verse, and some do not. The difference goes back to a discussion by some of the most eminent halakhic codifiers and commentators. *Tur* (*Oraḥ Ḥayyim*, 46) informs us that R. Yehuda he-Ḥasid, the most famous name of the medieval

German pietists, the Ḥasidei Ashkenaz, would add the Barukh shem kevod at this point and reasons that he did this because he intended thereby to fulfill the requirement of Reading the Shema in its proper time. The implication is clear: absence of the Barukh shem kevod means that we are simply relating something about the first verse, the Shema, but not reciting it as a fulfillment of the mitzvah obligation. Reciting the traditional verse means that the biblical verse is not merely a quotation, or a text for study, but is recited in fulfillment of the mitzvah of the Reading of the Shema. Now, for the Ziditchover there is no organic connection between the two verses; the second is an appendage, in the nature of a supplication, and does not innately relate to the biblical verse. For R. Shneur Zalman and R. Ḥayyim, however, the two are indissolubly connected; indeed, one without the other is either a distortion or meaningless. For the Ziditchover, therefore, the recitation or non-recitation of Barukh shem kevod following the Shema is irrelevant to the problem of whether the Shema Yisrael verse is a mere quote or the fulfillment of an obligation. For the other two, the matter is certainly critical: if, as did R. Yehuda he-Ḥasid, we recite the Barukh shem kevod and that indicates the desire to fulfill a formal mitzvah (that of the Reading of the Shema), whereas the absence of the traditional verse reduces the whole passage to the level of a citation and nothing more, then the traditional verse is critical to the full import of the biblical one.The Tur, therefore, would constitute prima facie proof for R. Shneur Zalman and R. Ḥayyim against the Ziditchover. Proponents of the Ziditchover view can manage to find counter-evidence in the writings of the commentators on both the Tur and the relevant comment of Rema in Shulḥan Arukh (Oraḥ Ḥayyim, 46), but the text of the Tur itself would indicate a predisposition in favor of the tighter connection between the two verses. Again, this is not a decisive halakhic proof by any means—certainly not sufficient to justify the extravagant claims cited above on behalf of the acosmic interpretation—but should be considered in evaluating a halakhic position on the issue. In general, one gets the feeling that the Halakha issued guidelines rather than legal rulings in regard to the content of required meditations and of spirituality in general.

Chapter 8

1. Eugene Borowitz has written about this briefly in his introductory chapter to the book he edited, *Echad: The Many Meanings of God is One* (New York: Sh'ma, 1988).
2. I elaborate upon this divergence of views between Saadia and Maimonides in my article, "The Unity of God and the Unity of the World: Saadia and Maimonides," in *Torah and Wisdom: Studies in Jewish Philosophy, Kabbalah, and Halacha—Essays in Honor of Arthur Hyman,* ed. Ruth Link-Salinger (New York: Sheugold Publishing, 1992), pp. 113–8.
3. Saadia, *The Book of Beliefs and Opinions,* trans. Samuel Rosenblatt (New Haven: Yale University Press, 1948), Treatise X, p. 357f.
4. Maimonides, *Guide for the Perplexed,* part I, chapter 72. I have used here a combination of the newer translation by Shlomo Pines (Chicago: University of Chicago Press, 1963), pp. 184–91, and the older one by M. Friedlander (New York: Hebrew Publishing Co., 2nd ed., 1956), pp. 113–8. For more on Maimonides' view, see my *Faith and Doubt,* chapter 2, n. 1.
5. Michael Berenbaum, *The New Polytheism,* cited in Borowitz, op. cit., p. 1.
6. The terms are those of Daniel J. Elazar, in Borowitz, p. 33.
7. I have devoted an entire volume to this subject. See my *Torah Umadda: The Encounter of Religious Learning and Worldly Knowledge in the Jewish Tradition* (Northvale, N.J. and London: Jason Aronson Inc., 1990), especially chapters 8, 9, 10, and 13.

Chapter 9

1. The verse permits a number of different translations. The late Dr. Philip Birnbaum, for instance, insists upon "Blessed be the name

of His glorious *majesty* forever and ever" (see his *Ha-Siddur ha-Shalem* [New York: Hebrew Publishing Co., 1949], introduction, p. xvi). But because this and other translations do not affect our theme substantively, we shall forego any detailed attempt at a more accurate translation.

2. This may explain why the verse is recited after pronouncing a doubtful blessing, i.e., if one is in doubt whether it is obligatory to recite a *berakha*. To forego the blessing, if it is indeed required, is to refrain knowingly from blessing God when the Halakha demands it; to recite it when it is not required is to violate the commandment not to take the Lord's Name in vain. The responsive nature of the liturgical sanctification is first mentioned in Sifre (to *Haazinu*, 32), giving other illustrations and offering biblical warrant. See my *Halakhot ve'Halikhot*, pp. 39–41.

3. R. Eliezer of Worms, quoted by the biblical exegete R. Bahya in his commentary to Deut. 6:4; and see Jerusalem Talmud, cited in *Yalkut Shimoni* to *Va-et'hanan*, 836.

4. Interestingly, confirmation of these three central points that Shema and *Barukh shem kevod* have in common comes from an analysis of the *Atta hu* paragraph recited after the very first reading of the Shema at the beginning of the morning service (the *keriat shema de'korbanot*). See too in *Iyyun Tefillah* in *Siddur Otzar ha-Tefillot*, who noticed the relationship of this passage to *Barukh shem kevod* without explicating it. It can be argued that this seems to be in accord with the Ziditchover as opposed to the R. Shneur Zalman–R. Hayyim interpretation. This is supported especially by the last four words of the passage, which are in the form of a supplication, thus bearing out the view of the Ziditchover that *Barukh shem kevod* is essentially a prayer rather than an affirmation or proclamation of a tenet of faith.

5. However, the Gemara obviously did not know or approve of it, otherwise the dialogue between R. Jeremiah and R. Aha b. Jacob hardly makes sense.

6. A play on the word *tzevi*, a "roe" or "deer," and *tzava*, "the heavenly or angelic hosts."

7. Again a play on words: *besamim,* "spices," and *ba-shamayim,* "in the heavens."
8. Song of Songs Rabbah, 8:13, 14.
9. Deuteronomy Rabbah, paragraph 2.
10. The four times are as follows: the two times mandated halakhically, namely, the Shema as part of the morning *(Shaharit)* service and the evening *(Maariv)* service; the Shema recited before the reading of the sacrificial order *(korbanot)* as part of the preliminaries to *Shaharit;* and the Shema recited before retiring at night *(keriat shema she'al ha-mittah).*

Chapter 10

1. Reprinted, with changes, from *Maimonidean Studies,* vol. 3 (1994).
2. "All the Torah is included in the commandment to love God, because he who loves the King devotes all his thoughts to doing that which is good and right in His eyes" *(Sefer Mitzvot Gadol,* Positive Commandment 3).
3. The most comprehensive work on this subject is that of George Vajda, *L'amour De Dieu Dans La Theologie Juive Du Moyen Age* (Paris: Jo Vrin, 1957). When I published my article on which this chapter is based in *Maimonidean Studies* in 1993, I was unaware of the excellent article by Shubert Spero, "Maimonides and Our Love for God," in *Judaism* (Summer 1983), 32:3.
4. *Sefer ha-Mitzvot,* Positive Commandment 2.
5. This analysis of love and fear of God should be compared with that of the nineteenth-century Protestant thinker Rudolf Otto, who, in his *The Idea of the Holy,* wrote of two reactions to Nature; the first is *fascination* with the divine wisdom implicit in Nature, and the second is *terror* as man retreats before the *Mysterium Tremendum.* I do not know if Maimonides influenced him directly, but he certainly preceded Otto in this almost identical formulation.
6. The role of intuition is significant in the works of Maimonides. In the introduction to the *Guide,* he speaks of momentary flashes

of intuition—unmediated by any cognitive act—as both the mode of apprehension of metaphysical knowledge and of prophecy. This epistemology, of course, presents a problem because of Maimonides' high esteem for metaphysical deduction and clear, logical analysis. Julius Guttmann, who raises this issue, offers no solution; see his *Philosophies of Judaism*, trans. David W. Silverman (Philadelphia: Jewish Publication Society, 1964), pp. 156f. The most obvious answer, however, is provided by a close reading of our key passage. Here, Maimonides does not speak of the intuitive (*mi-yad*, "immediately") reaction as the first response to Nature, but the second. Thus, the love for God comes about after one "contemplates" the wonders of creation and "sees" in them the infinite wisdom of the Divine, and only then does he "immediately" love Him, etc. The same pattern holds for the fear of God: when man "considers" these matters, i.e., the wonders of creation, he "immediately" withdraws into himself in fear, etc. What we have here is a two-step process: first one studies Nature; *then* this evokes the latent intuitive response of the appropriate religious emotions. Hence, the study of natural science leads to the intuitive reaction of love and fear to the creation. It is later left for the philosopher to elaborate on these responses in the language of metaphysics. This philosophical elaboration, too, involves a flash of insight that is, however, different from the love and fear reactions; it is, as it were, a "normal" epistemological act and one that must then be set down according to all the rules of metaphysical argument.

7. *Sefer ha-Mitzvot,* Positive Commandment 3.

8. *Sefer ha-Ḥinukh,* 418.

9. See note 3.

10. There is no justification for the inclusion of Torah alongside Nature as the source of love and fear by reading this into the closing phrase of Maimonides in his *Hilkhot Yesodei Ha-Torah,* cited above, or as an addition to it. The same uncertainty about the correct interpretation of the Sifre will be noticed in the comment of Netziv in his *Haamek Davar* to Deut. 6:7, especially in the addenda to this commentary taken from the author's manu-

script. In the commentary proper he cites the Sifre and takes it clearly to imply that the study of Torah is the means to achieve the love for God. In the addenda, however, he concedes that the plain sense of the Sifre passage would indicate that the contemplation of the creation and Nature are the vehicles to *ahavat Hashem* and that Maimonides, in the above passage from *Hilkhot Yesodei ha-Torah,* supports that understanding. However, the Netziv adds, one cannot derive *ahavat Hashem* from the study of Nature alone; such exclusive contemplation may well lead to an appreciation of the greatness of the Creator, but hardly to *loving* Him. It may be compared to one who knows *that* another person is great and worthy of love, but he does not know *him* personally, so that even if he sees him he cannot love him because he does not truly *know* him. So, the study of natural science can lead to love only if it is preceded by the study of Torah, for then, to continue the analogy, one knows the other person directly and can then learn to love him. Note the intellectual honesty and also the breadth of Netziv's own approach—he points to the inadequacy of Nature as a source of *ahavat Hashem* without disqualifying it altogether and recommends that both study of science and study of Torah together provide the entree to love for God, with Torah taking priority over science (a point he makes often; see e.g., op. cit. to Deut. 4:2). Such breadth and intellectual capaciousness, with the accompanying sensitivity to complexity and subtle nuances, should not be confused with the kind of ambivalence that bespeaks an inability to make up one's mind for fear of making the wrong choice. For more on the attitude of Netziv on this issue, see my *Torah Umadda,* pp. 40–1, 44, and 72, note 2. Also see Hannah Katz, *Mishnat ha-Netziv* (Jerusalem: n.p., 1990), pp. 109–16; however, her use of the term "ambivalent" for Netziv's breadth of scope and sensitivity to complexity is unfortunate because it implies indecisiveness, which clearly was not part of Netziv's personality.

11. In the very beginning of the *Guide* (introduction to part I), Maimonides holds that the deeper understanding of the Torah, which he identifies with philosophic truth, is available to the

NOTES TO PAGE 85

intellectual elite and is not to be revealed to ordinary people. However, this does not result in disdain for the "benighted masses"; the latter are granted, in simple and uncomplicated fashion, certain basic truths, such as the incorporeality of God. Thus, Maimonides (like Onkelos) held that the figurative interpretation of biblical anthropomorphisms and anthropopathisms must be taught to all Jews regardless of their intellectual sophistication or lack of it.

12. The elite, however, must continue to abide by the actional commandments along with ordinary people; their higher aspirations and deeper understanding are not a dispensation to do away with the obligations that devolve upon all other Jews. Everything in the life and writings of Maimonides rejects the notion, sometimes proposed, that the elite are beyond the law.

13. The study of Nature (which is the prerequisite for the intuitive reactions of love and fear, as mentioned above) is far less esoteric than philosophical speculation. The Talmud *requires* one who is capable of studying geometry and astronomy to do so, and "one who knows how to calculate the cycles and planetary courses but does not do so, of him Scripture says," citing Isa. 5:12, "but they regard not the work of the Lord, nor have they considered the work of His hands" (*Shabbat* 75a). We find no direct talmudic encouragement of the study of philosophy as such. Maimonides (who asserts that his interpretation of a talmudic text is warrant for his view on the study of metaphysics; see below) raises philosophy to the highest rung in the religious life, higher than that of the natural sciences. Thus, after introducing chapter 2 of the "Laws of the Foundations of the Torah" by stating the source of love and fear, Maimonides undertakes to teach the reader about matter and form, the angels, the nature of divine knowledge, divine unity, etc. All this, he says (2:11) is included in the term *maaseh merkavah*, the highly esoteric study of Ezekiel's "divine chariot." The next two chapters deal with astronomy and physics. "All these matters are only a drop in the bucket and deep, but not as profound as [the matters taken up in] the first two chapters." The latter two chapters are referred to as *maaseh*

bereshit, literally, the acts of genesis, which, while they are not popular fare, are not as recondite and restricted as is the study of *maaseh merkavah* (4:10, 11). Hence, the study of Nature is available, even required, of those who have the talent for it, but not for all others, while the study of philosophy is clearly reserved for those who have both the aptitude and the spiritual preparation for it. See too R. Isaac Simha Hurewitz, *Yad Levi* (Commentary to Maimonides' *Sefer ha-Mitzvot*), Shoresh 1, no. 40 (Jerusalem: n.p., 1927), pp. 18a, b.

14. *Hilkhot Yesodei ha-Torah,* 2:2, end.
15. Ibid., 4:10. See too n. 12.
16. Ibid., 4:13.
17. See the commentary to Maimonides' *Sefer ha-Mitzvot* by R. Hananiah b. Menahem, *Kin'at Soferim* (Livorno: n.p., 1740), Positive Commandment 3.

Chapter 11

1. *Netivot Olam, Netiv Koah ha-Yetzer,* chapter 4.
2. See Nahmanides' commentary on the Torah, to Exod. 20:8.
3. Maharal, *Netivot Olam, Netiv Yirat Hashem,* chapter 1. What motivates this interpretation is the author's awareness that Abraham is usually presented as the archetype of God-lover rather than God-fearer; see Isa. 41:8, 2 Chron. 20:7.
4. It is interesting to compare this structuring of fear by Maharal to a similar dichotomy in the analysis of love by R. Bahya Ibn Pakuda (c. 1050–c. 1156) in the last section of his *Hovot ha-Levavot* ("Duties of the Heart"). Bahya holds that the love for God is the acme of all religious life, and all other virtues are prerequisite for and preparatory to it. There are two kinds of love, he avers: The lower kind, accessible to most humans, derives from fear. The higher kind, which is independent of fear and of any intended personal benefit, material or spiritual, is reserved for the elite who are prepared to surrender everything, including life itself, for the love of God. Even then, such love is granted to these

few individuals only as an act of divine grace; see chapters 4–6 of *Hovot ha-Levavot*.

5. See chapter 7.
6. *Netivot Olam, Netiv Ahavat Hashem*, chapter 1.
7. Ibid.
8. *Netivot Olam, Netiv Ahavat Hashem*, chapter 1.
9. Ibid.

Chapter 12

1. What follows is largely based upon Mordechai Teitelbaum's *Ha-Rav mi-Ladi u-Mifleget Habad* (Warsaw: Tushiyah, 1910–13). For more on Hasidism's conceptions of love of God, se my *Religious Thought of Hasidism* (in progress), chap. 4.
2. *Tikkunei Zohar*, 10: "Torah without the two wings of fear and love does not fly upwards."
3. Compare this with the Maharal's view on the "naturalness" of religious feeling and expression; see chapter 11.
4. This definition of *ahavat olam* by R. Shneur Zalman is based upon the equivocal meaning of *olam*. In biblical Hebrew it means "forever," and that indeed is how the term is conventionally translated: an eternal love. In rabbinic Hebrew, however, the word *olam* changes from a time- to a space-oriented meaning: world rather than eternity. It is this latter meaning that R. Shneur Zalman attributes to it.

Chapter 13

1. See his *Tzidkat ha-Tzaddik*, no. 200. Note that the terms *ahavah rabbah* and *ahavat olam* are used in the last blessing before the reading of the Shema, one in the morning and the other in the evening (according to some versions; for others, only *ahavah rabbah* is recited).
2. R. Zadok may be intending a wordplay: *olam* in biblical Hebrew means "forever," and Kabbalists use it to signify the relation to

he'elam, hiddenness or concealment, because *ahavat olam* is of a far lower emotional temperature than *ahavah rabbah*.

3. *Tzidkat ha-Tzaddik,* 196.

4. R. Zadok's use of the term "love of Israel" for a generation that long preceded the emergence of Israel as a people is not an anachronism due to the author's oversight. It does indicate, rather, that the term *ahavat Yisrael,* the love of Israel, is a paradigm for love of humankind; otherwise, this entire passage makes no sense. Similarly, as we shall see presently, he uses the term "Torah" for knowledge in general.

5. In his *Peri Tzaddik,* vol. III, *Kedoshim,* p. 74b.

6. This, of course, is reminiscent of Maimonides' original distinction between love and fear as representing, respectively, the outgoing, centrifugal quest for God and His wisdom, and the centripetal motion of withdrawal and retreat as the reaction of awe to the divine power; see chapter 10.

Chapter 14

1. *Guide for the Perplexed,* 3:28.

2. *Hilkhot Yesodei ha-Torah,* chapters 2–4.

3. For a more elaborate discussion on this controversy between Maimonides and Ramban (Naḥmanides), see my "Loving and Hating Jews as Halakhic Categories," in *Tradition* (Winter, 1989), pp. 102–4 and notes thereon.

Chapter 15

1. The fullest treatment of the subject is by Abraham Joshua Heschel in his *God in Search of Man* (New York: Meridian Books, 1966, pp. 75, 252, and elsewhere) and, in lesser measure, in some of his earlier works.

2. See, on this, my *Faith and Doubt* (New York: Ktav, 1971), pp. 32–4.

3. To *Shevuot,* ad loc.

4. See *Yalkut* to Isaiah 63, no. 507.
5. See my article on "Kiddush Hashem" in the *Encyclopedia Judaica,* vol. X, pp. 978–82 for references.
6. *Mi-pinkas Zikhronotai* (Jerusalem: n.p., 1987), p. 23f.
7. God as *eḥad* (one) is frequently referred to in the Jerusalem Talmud (*Megillah* 10a) and midrashic literature (Genesis Rabbah, 1:12, 98:13, and elsewhere) as *yaḥid* (individual, singular) or *yeḥido shel olam* (He who is singular in the world). This quality of aloneness is akin to, and implies, loneliness; hence the verse in Ps. 25:16, "Turn unto me and be gracious unto me; *ki yaḥid ve-'ani ani,* for I am solitary and afflicted." The connection between *yaḥid* and *'ani,* afflicted, surely points to a painful loneliness of the Psalmist. By extension, the singularity and aloneness of God suggest loneliness.
8. The words of Erwin Altman (1908–1989), dictated to his brother Manfred, as cited by Levi Meier in his *Jewish Values in Psychotherapy: Essays on Vital Issues on the Search for Meaning* (Lanham / New York / London: University Press of America, 1988), p. 161.
9. This sharing of solitude illustrates the mutual sympathy between God and humanity. Other such instances of solicitude for divine solitude may be cited from the world of literature. As an example, one of the greatest of contemporary Hebrew poets, the late Uri Zvi Greenberg, is the author of an intriguing poem entitled "The Great Sadness" (or: "The Great Sad One"), which at first appears intended solely as pixyish or even as biting, mocking humor but really conveys as well a sense of sympathy for God, who, in His oneness, suffers loneliness. The divine sadness issues from His solitude, having no close, intimate friend. A human can at least exchange body warmth with another, can smoke a cigar and drink a cup of coffee or glass of wine, can sleep and dream until dawn; but that is unavailable to Him—for He is God. . . . See too Sherry H. Blumberg, "Eḥad: God's Unity" in *Eḥad: The Many Meanings of God Is One,* ed. Eugene Borowitz (n.p.: Sh'ma, 1988), p. 9.
10. See the beginning of chapter 12.

11. See his *The Body of Faith: Judaism as Corporeal Election* (New York: Seabury Press, 1983), pp. 13, 60–5, and 119–24. One need not accept Wyschogrod's entire thesis in order to appreciate his contribution to a broader and more existentially meaningful conception of Judaism's understanding of love between God and man.

Chapter 16

1. Sifre to Deuteronomy, *pesikta* 32.
2. The homiletic interpretation is based upon the use of *levavkha* rather than *libkha*. Both mean the same thing, "your heart," though one is spelled with one *bet* and the other with two of them (see *Tiferet Yisrael* to *Berakhot* 9:5). The extra *bet* is significant because this letter has the numerical value of two, as the second letter of the Hebrew alphabet. Hence—two Urges. An alternative explanation is that the word *be'khol*, "with *all* your heart," is here being expounded and is meant to include the Evil Urge (see Zohar, 3:267a).
3. It is worth noting that this conception became the cornerstone of Hasidism's view of evil in the world. Indeed, the Baal Shem Tov often spoke of evil as "a seat for the good" or as "a vehicle for the good," i.e., a *means* to a good, or greater good. See my *Religious Thought of Hasidism,* chap. 15. Developing and expanding on his predecessor's theme, R. Zadok Hakohen explicitly identifies evil as contingent and relative:

> One must not think of all the potencies implanted in the Jewish soul that they are evil and that one must strive for their opposites, for there is no quality that does not possess some dimension of the good as well. But one must use it in accordance with the will of God; for if it does not accord with His will, then even the good qualities are evil. That is why King Saul was punished for exercising compassion.

R. Zadok cites our midrash as a source for his conclusion that evil is not intrinsic and "real" and that the convertibility of good and evil depends ultimately on intention and context. This highly optimistic vision of human nature found in hasidic thought, so characteristic of the whole of the hasidic world-view, presents us with a fairly simple theodicy—simple, that is, as long as we do not examine too closely the empirical record of history, particularly of the middle of the twentieth century, which raises many troubling problems.

4. *Tanya*, 1:27.

5. I recall a lecture by my late teacher, Rabbi Joseph B. Soloveitchik, o.b.m., in which he explained the Mishnah (*Avot* 4:1), "Who is mighty? He who suppresses his passions." He avers that this is a minimalist, not a maximalist position. The higher achievement is not the suppression *(kibbush)* but the sanctification *(kiddush)* of the *yetzer*. These terms are analogous, respectively, to R. Shneur Zalman's *itkafia* and *it'hapkha*.

6. Commentary on the Mishnah to *Berakhot* 9:1.

7. *Berakhot* 63a.

8. *Netivot Olam, Netiv Ahavat Hashem*, 1:39–41.

9. In his collection of short stories, *Short Friday* (Philadelphia: Jewish Publication Society of America, 1965).

10. An alternative to the translation of *me'odekha* as "your might" is "your money" or possessions (Sifre to *Va-et'hanan*, 32:7, and *Berakhot* 61b); see later in this chapter.

11. *Shaar ha-Otiot*, end of letter alef.

12. *Harḥev Davar* to Deut. 6:5, no. 2.

13. *Eruvin* 21b.

14. R. Baruch Epstein, *Torah Temimah* to Deut. 6:5, no. 22.

15. Mishnah *Berakhot* 9:1 and Gemara *Berakhot* 61b.

16. This second interpretation is a variation on the theme of "one must bless God for the bad [news] as well as for the good" (Mishnah *Berakhot* 9:1; see too *Berakhot* 33b). In a sense, this more imaginative interpretation may be a further example of "very-ness," in that we must love God in all extremes of emotion—whether *very* happy or *very* sad.

17. Both in their respective commentaries to Deut. 6:5.
18. In similar fashion, R. Shneur Zalman explains the rabbinic dictum that the mitzvah of charity *(tzedakah)* is equivalent to all the other commandments put together by saying that a man's material means are gained at the expense of all his effort and toil and labor, indeed the very juices of his life; hence when he shares this with those less fortunate, he is giving them not just alms but his "vital soul," part of his very self. See his *Tanya,* 1:37.
19. *Torah Temimah* to Deut. 6:5.
20. Rema to *Shulḥan Arukh, Oraḥ Ḥayyim,* 248:16.
21. *Magen Avraham,* commentary to *Shulḥan Arukh, Oraḥ Ḥayyim,* 248:16.
22. In *Torah Temimah* to Deut. 6:5, no. 24, he offers the following insight as support: The words *be'khol me'odkha* are mentioned in the singular ("your") in the first paragraph of the Shema, but the parallel plural, *be'khol me'odkhem,* "with all *your* (plural) might/money," is omitted in the next paragraph of the Shema, where it belongs for reasons of symmetry after "with all your (plural) heart" and "with all your (plural) soul." The reason for this omission, he suggests, is that the first paragraph has as its theme "the accepting of the yoke of the Kingdom of Heaven," the very essence of the first verse of the Shema and its implied denial of idolatry. Now, idolatry is one of the three cardinal sins, and here the sacrifice of one's possessions is equivalent to the sacrifice of one's very life. However, the second paragraph deals with the mitzvot in general—"And it shall come to pass if you will listen carefully to My *commandments,*" etc.—and one is not required to sacrifice all one's worldly goods for transgressions other than the cardinal three—just as one need not suffer martyrdom for them. However, this interpretation comes to grief because of the fact that the second paragraph of the Shema does contain the command to love God "with all your heart" and "with all your soul." To be consistent, that would have to imply the necessity for martyrdom even in minor cases, such as the other negative commandments, which, however, is certainly not the case. R. Epstein is aware of the question, but his answer is

far from adequate. He writes: in this second paragraph, the two elements of heart and soul are not meant to serve as Halakha, directing the offering up of one's life, but rather as a general expression of intent and love in serving the Creator. This, however, again violates simple consistency, for then "with all your money" could be explained in the same way—as hortatory rather than halakhic.

23. R. Zadok Hakohen, *Tzidkat ha-Tzaddik*, 86.
24. Ibid.
25. R. Zadok Hakohen, *Tzidkat ha-Tzaddik*, 197.
26. Ibid, 86.

Chapter 17

1. *Shulḥan Arukh, Oraḥ Ḥayyim*, 60:5; and see appendix.
2. Midrash Aggada, Gen. 2:2.
3. These remarks are culled from his *Tzidkat ha-Tzaddik*, 210.
4. No. 418. Also cited in *Mishnah Berurah*, 1.
5. Sifre to *Va-et'ḥanan*, 8.
6. See chapter 10 for a more elaborate discussion on this theme.
7. See above, n. 6.
8. Midrash Tanḥuma (Warsaw ed.), to Noaḥ, chapter 3.
9. The same question appears in Tosafot (to *Shabbat* 88a, s.v. *Kafah*), which apparently was unaware of the passage in the *Tanḥuma*.
10. Paraphrasing Song of Songs 8:6.
11. *Ve'shinantam* ("you shall teach them diligently") is related to *shinun*, sharpness or acuity, i.e., the kind of study that requires keen logical analysis.
12. See Ibn Ezra, ad loc., who refers to Prov. 25:18, *ḥetz shanun*, "a sharp arrow."
13. See also *Kiddushin* 30a, where other interpretations are suggested, relating to the individual (adult) student, that he should be methodical in his study and remember the material so that if he is asked for the law, he should not hesitate but should be pre-

pared to answer immediately and clearly. (The source for this talmudic text is the Sifre to *Va-et'hanan*, 9.)

14. Sifre to *Va-et'hanan*, 9.
15. Zohar III, 268a.
16. *Raya Mehemna* to *Yitro*, 93a.
17. Rashi, ad loc. See too in Rabbenu Hananel, ad loc.
18. Tosafot, s.v. *Bam*. An earlier source is the Jerusalem Talmud,
    Berakhot 2:1, end, and 4:4.
19. Rashi, ad loc. The problem with Rashi's interpretation is that it
    makes Rava's statement redundant. See too Midrash Psalms,
    39:4.
20. Rabbenu Hananel, ad loc. This view is cited as well by R. Nathan
    of Rome in his *Arukh*, s.v. *Bam*; see *Arukh ha-Shalem*, p. 107.
21. Sifre to *Va-et'hanan*, 9. Apparently, the Sifre uses this verse to dis-
    approve of any secular study. Yet, its formulation of Torah being
    major and not secondary would imply that profane or worldly
    study is permissible as long as it is secondary to Torah study.
    One must always study Torah; even if one engages in "the wis-
    dom of the nations of the world," Torah remains primary and
    must never be neglected or relegated to secondary status. What-
    ever the case, R. Aha's statement in the Talmud is, as stated,
    milder and less radical.
22. *Arukh*, s.v. *Bam*; see *Arukh ha-Shalem*, p. 107.
23. *Netivot Olam*, II, p. 98; *Netiv ha-Shetikah*, chapter I.
24. *Ha'amek Davar* to Deut. 6:7.
25. *Hilkhot Teshuvah*, 10:3.
26. *Sukkah* 25a, and *Berakhot* 11a.
27. Pseudo-Jonathan to Deut. 6:7. Some commentators have sug-
    gested that the *Targum* sides with those authorities who, citing
    Mishnah *Berakhot* 2:5 that Rabban Gamaliel himself recited the
    Shema on his wedding night, hold that a groom should recite the
    Shema.
28. Zohar III, p. 269a. It is possible that the Zohar plays on the
    word *ve'dibbarta* ("you shall talk"): the root *d-b-r* in Hebrew
    means "talk" or "speak" and in Aramaic means "lead" or "con-
    duct." On the talmudic attitude on the manner of conducting

one's household, see my *"Sheloshah Devarim ..."* in *Hapardes* (Kislev, 5754).

29. Mishnah *Berakhot* 1:3.

30. Ibid.

31. *Tzidkat ha-Tzaddik, 3.*

32. This last clause is a quotation from Rema, in his very first gloss to the first volume of the *Shulḥan Arukh, Oraḥ Ḥayyim.* It is, in turn, a paraphrase of the talmudic dictum directed to the worshiper who stands before the Almighty to recite the *Amidah,* "Know before Whom you stand" (*Berakhot* 28b).

33. *Horeb,* trans. Dayan I. Grunfled (London: 1962), vol. I, p. 179.

34. *Naḥaliel* (Jerusalem: Mosad Harav Kook, 1982), p. 125.

35. Hilkhot Mezuzah, 6:13.

36. *Tzeror ha-Mor* to *Va-et'ḥanan,* s.v. *Ve'amar ve'hayu.*

Appendix

1. Modern English, as well as most modern Western languages, differentiates between *reading—a private, individual act—and* reciting, which is generally a public act; the former may be done silently, the latter is always aloud. In Hebrew, however, the root *k-r-a* means both reading and reciting, perhaps because in antiquity the two were fused. The *keriah* of the Shema must likewise be understood as both reading and reciting; indeed, the Talmud specifically requires that it must be pronounced aloud "so that one's ears hear what he says" (although *post factum,* if it was read silently, it need not be repeated in order to fulfill one's obligation). We shall therefore be using the terms "reading" and "recitation" of the Shema interchangeably, but always with the idea that it is to be articulated audibly.

2. *Berakhot* 21a.

3. *Oraḥ Ḥayyim,* 67.

4. See their respective comments to *Berakhot* 21a.

5. There is some doubt about this, because Rambam is not explicit on the matter. See *Hilkhot Keriat Shema,* 1:2; and see *Peri Hadash, Oraḥ Ḥayyim,* 67, and *Shaagat Aryeh, Hilkhot Keriat*

Shema, 2.

6. *Berakhot* 13a.

7. I recall hearing this lecture, which was published later in his *Sheurim li'Zekher Abba Mari zal* (Jerusalem: 1983), vol. I, pp. 20ff.

8. *Hilkhot Keriat Shema,* 1:2.

9. Interestingly, the *Shulḥan Arukh* (*Oraḥ Ḥayyim,* 70:1) decides that women are exempt from the obligation to recite the Shema, but "it is proper to teach them to accept upon themselves the yoke of Heaven," upon which R. Moshe Isserles (Rema) adds the gloss, "they must read at least the first verse." The *Shulḥan Arukh* is obviously speaking of the mitzvah of *yiḥud Hashem* (thus his use of *kabbalat 'ol malkhut shamayim,* "accepting the yoke of the Kingdom of Heaven") when he affirms the desirability of women reciting the Shema, whereas the Rema adds the obligation of *keriah,* that of reading the Shema as well. But, asks R. Mordecai Yaffe, author of *Levush* (No. 70), is not the reading of the Shema a time-bound mitzvah and should not, therefore, women be exempt? His answer is that Rema intended the mitzvah of *yiḥud Hashem,* which certainly does obligate women, and it is the recitation of the Shema that gives them a defined opportunity to fulfill that mitzvah, even though the mitzvah of recitation per se does not apply to them.

10. The second of the two benedictions preceding the Shema in both the morning and evening service is considered a *birkhat ha-mitzvah*—a blessing over the performance of a commandment, the commandment in this case being that of the Reading of the Shema. Indeed, if one failed to recite this prior blessing, which is a fixed part of the daily liturgy, R. Amram Gaon (cited by Rosh, beginning of *Berakhot*) requires the recitation of a special benediction, "Blessed are You . . . who has commanded us concerning the reading of the Shema."

11. For a more detailed exposition of this theme, see my *Halakhot ve'Halikhot,* chapter 3.

Index